D1124336

Chemistry Experiments

FACTS ON FILE
SCIENCE EXPERIMENTS

Chemistry Experiments

Pamela Walker
Elaine Wood

An imprint of Infobase Publishing

Chemistry Experiments

Facts On File, Inc.
An imprint of Infobase Publishing
132 West 31st Street
New York NY 10001

Library of Congress Cataloging-in-Publication Data
Walker, Pam, 1958-
Chemistry experiments / Pamela Walker, Elaine Wood.
p. cm. — (Facts on file Science experiments)
Includes bibliographical references and index.
ISBN 978-0-8160-8172-1
1. Chemistry–Experiments–Juvenile literature. 2. Chemistry –Study and teaching (Middle school) –Activity programs. 3. Chemistry –Study and teaching (Secondary) –Activity programs. I. Wood, Elaine, 1950- II. Title.
QD43.W324 2011
540.78–dc22
2010033149

Editor: Frank K. Darmstadt
Copy Editor: Betsy Feist at A Good Thing, Inc.
Project Coordinator: Aaron Richman
Art Director: Howard Petlack
Production: Victoria Kessler
Illustrations: Hadel Studios
Cover printed by: Bang Printing, Brainerd, MN
Book printed and bound by Bang Printing, Brainerd, MN
Date printed: December 2010
Printed in the United States of America

10 9 8 7 6 5 4 3 2 1

This book is printed on acid-free paper.

Contents

Preface vii

Acknowledgments xi

Introduction xiii

Safety Precautions xvii

  1. The Smell of an Ester 1

  2. The Chemistry of Toothpaste 9

  3. Water Softeners 16

  4. Lewis Structures 24

  5. Making Soap 32

  6. Ozone Depletion 40

  7. Catalysis of Hydrogen Peroxide 47

  8. Wood Alcohol 54

  9. Solutes Affect the Boiling Point of Water 60

10. Potable Water 67

11. Solutions and Spectrophotometry 74

12. Endothermic and Exothermic Reactions 81

13. Finding Molar Mass 88

14. Chemical Moles 96

15. Heat Energy 102

16. Chloride Levels 110

17. The Rate of Rusting 117

18. Thin Layer Chromatography 123

19. Levels of Sugar 131

20. Microscale Percent Composition 138

Scope and Sequence Chart 144

Grade Level 146

Setting 147

Our Findings 148

Glossary 167

Internet Resources 172

Periodic Table of Elements 175

Index 176

Preface

For centuries, humans have studied and explored the natural world around them. The ever-growing body of knowledge resulting from these efforts is science. Information gained through science is passed from one generation to the next through an array of educational programs. One of the primary goals of every science education program is to help young people develop critical-thinking and problem-solving skills that they can use throughout their lives.

Science education is unique in academics in that it not only conveys facts and skills; it also cultivates curiosity and creativity. For this reason, science is an active process that cannot be fully conveyed by passive teaching techniques. The question for educators has always been, "What is the best way to teach science?" There is no simple answer to this question, but studies in education provide useful insights.

Research indicates that students need to be actively involved in science, learning it through experience. Science students are encouraged to go far beyond the textbook and to ask questions, consider novel ideas, form their own predictions, develop experiments or procedures, collect information, record results, analyze findings, and use a variety of resources to expand knowledge. In other words, students cannot just hear science; they must also do science.

"Doing" science means performing experiments. In the science curriculum, experiments play a number of educational roles. In some cases, hands-on activities serve as hooks to engage students and introduce new topics. For example, a discrepant event used as an introductory experiment encourages questions and inspires students to seek the answers behind their findings. Classroom investigations can also help expand information that was previously introduced or cement new knowledge. According to neuroscience, experiments and other types of hands-on learning help transfer new learning from short-term into long-term memory.

Facts On File Science Experiments is a multivolume set of experiments that helps engage students and enable them to "do" science. The high-interest experiments in these books put students' minds into gear and give them opportunities to become involved, to think independently, and to build on their own base of science knowledge.

As a resource, Facts On File Science Experiments provides teachers with new and innovative classroom investigations that are presented in a clear, easy-to-understand style. The areas of study in this multivolume set include forensic science, environmental science, computer research, physical science, weather and climate, space and astronomy and many others. Experiments are supported by colorful figures and line illustrations that help hold students' attention and explain information. All of the experiments in these books use multiple science process skills such as observing, measuring, classifying, analyzing, and predicting. In addition, some of the experiments require students to practice inquiry science by setting up and carrying out their own open-ended experiments.

Each volume of the set contains 20 new experiments as well as extensive safety guidelines, glossary, correlation to the National Science Education Standards, scope and sequence, and an annotated list of Internet resources. An introduction that presents background information begins each investigation to provide an overview of the topic. Every experiment also includes relevant specific safety tips along with materials list, procedure, analysis questions, explanation of the experiment, connections to real life, and an annotated further reading section for extended research.

Pam Walker and Elaine Wood, the authors of Facts On File Science Experiments, are sensitive to the needs of both science teachers and students. The writing team has more than 40 years of combined science teaching experience. Both are actively involved in planning and improving science curricula in their home state, Georgia, where Pam was the 2007 Teacher of the Year. Walker and Wood are master teachers who hold specialist degrees in science and science education. They are the authors of dozens of books for middle and high school science teachers and students.

Facts On File Science Experiments, by Walker and Wood, facilitates science instruction by making it easy for teachers to incorporate experimentation. During experiments, students reap benefits that are not available in other types of instruction. One of these benefits is the opportunity to take advantage of the learning provided by social interactions. Experiments are usually carried out in small groups, enabling students to brainstorm and learn from each other. The validity of group work as an effective learning tool is supported by research in neuroscience, which shows that the brain is a social organ and that communication and collaboration are activities that naturally enhance learning.

Experimentation addresses many different types of learning, including lateral thinking, multiple intelligences, and constructivism. In lateral thinking, students solve problems using nontraditional methods. Long-established, rigid procedures for problem-solving are replaced by original ideas from students.

When encouraged to think laterally, students are more likely to come up with unique ideas that are not usually found in the traditional classroom. This type of thinking requires students to construct meaning from an activity and to think like scientists.

Another benefit of experimentation is that it accommodates students' multiple intelligences. According to the theory of multiple intelligences, students possess many different aptitudes, but in varying degrees. Some of these forms of intelligence include linguistic, musical, logical-mathematical, spatial, kinesthetic, intrapersonal, and interpersonal. Learning is more likely to be acquired and retained when more than one sense is involved. During an experiment, students of all intellectual types find roles in which they can excel.

Students in the science classroom become involved in active learning, constructing new ideas based on their current knowledge and their experimental findings. The constructivist theory of learning encourages students to discover principles for and by themselves. Through problem solving and independent thinking, students build on what they know, moving forward in a manner that makes learning real and lasting.

Active, experimental learning makes connections between newly acquired information and the real world, a world that includes jobs. In the 21st century, employers expect their employees to identify and solve problems for themselves. Therefore, today's students, workers of the near future, will be required to use higher-level thinking skills. Experience with science experiments provides potential workers with the ability and confidence to be problem solvers.

The goal of Walker and Wood in this multivolume set is to provide experiments that hook and hold the interest of students, teach basic concepts of science, and help students develop their critical-thinking skills. When fully immersed in an experiment, students can experience those "Aha!" moments, the special times when new information merges with what is already known and understanding breaks through. On these occasions, real and lasting learning takes place. The authors hope that this set of books helps bring more "Aha" moments into every science class.

Acknowledgments

This book would not exist were it not for our editor, Frank K. Darmstadt, who conceived and directed the project. Frank supervised the material closely, editing and making invaluable comments along the way. Betsy Feist of A Good Thing, Inc., is responsible for transforming our raw material into a polished and grammatically correct manuscript that makes us proud. Special thanks go to Jessica Muchnick, friend, coworker, and chemistry teacher, whose expertise guided us in this book.

Introduction

Chemistry is referred to as the "central science" for a very good reason: The world of chemistry deals with composition of matter, its characteristics, and its reactions. Since everything that exists in the world is made up of matter, chemistry is a broad field. An understanding of basic chemical principles provides a frame of reference for studies in biology, geology, astronomy, and physics.

To appreciate the role of chemistry, we begin by examining ourselves. In the bodies of humans and all living things, millions of chemical reactions take place continuously. One of the basic reactions is cellular respiration, which releases the energy found in the chemical bonds of food molecules. In the environment, the chemical reaction of photosynthesis provides food and oxygen for living things all over the planet. The growth and production of food is a chemistry-based field. Chemical processes yield the fabrics in our clothes, the carpets on our floors, and the paints on our walls. Chemistry is required to manufacture all of the products that we use daily from to soap to hand lotion.

To help students in grades 6 through 12 understand the basic concepts behind all of these chemical reactions, Facts On File Science Experiments presents *Chemistry Experiments,* a new book of 20 unique laboratory activities that gives teachers some fresh ideas for the chemistry class. The majority of the experiments in this volume relate to the chemistry of daily living, helping students see the connection between what they are studying and why they need to study it. This approach removes the seeming abstractness of science, making it more concrete and easier to conceptualize.

The activities in *Chemistry Experiments* use several approaches to gain student interest and simplify difficult concepts. Research shows that one way to help learners retain what they hear in the classroom is to give them learning choices. By providing options, students become engaged in the activity. Options also give students a feeling of control and require them to make a decision based on their own interests. Several of the experiments incorporate choices for students. In "The Smell of an Ester," a lesson on production of esters, students must relate the goals of the experiment to the scents and flavors that are commercially added to food and other products. Based on their own experiences, they select the esters they will produce in the laboratory. Students are also given choices in "Water Softeners," an experiment that looks at several methods of softening hard water.

Students are asked to think like analytical consumers in several experiments. In "Making Soap," students learn the chemistry of soap production, then use their knowledge to plan and produce a specific type of soap based on their preferences. In "The Chemistry of Toothpaste," students find out how consumer tests are carried out and learn the meaning of chemicals listed on product labels. *Potable Water* challenges students to determine which of several chemical approaches is best in cleaning water. In "Heat Energy," students find out that not all fuels are the same and compare the heat per mole of several type of fuel. "Chloride Levels" looks at the effectiveness of water purifiers, specifically in relation to the amount of chlorine in water samples, using the technique of titration. "Thin Layer Chromatography" is an experiment in which students test the purity of over-the-counter analgesics. In "Levels of Sugar," students compare the amounts of sugar listed on fruit juice labels to sugar contents they find experimetally.

Gaining the technical skills needed in a chemistry laboratory helps students succeed in their work and provides them with the skills needed later to design their own experiments. For this reason, several experiments teach basic lab skills that have wide application. These procedures are useful in other experiments. "Microscale Percent Composition" for example, demonstrates an experimentation technique that conserves resources and is used to compare the amount of carbonation in different beverages. "Catalysis of Hydrogen Peroxide" shows students how to carry out titration while gaining an understanding of the chemistry behind catalysts. Distillation is demonstrated in "Wood Alcohol," an experiment in which students produce this common household chemical. Spectrometry, a technique that can be used for analyzing the composition of compounds, is taught in "Solutions and Spectrophotometry." "Finding Molar Mass" relates the abstract concepts of chemical formulas and molar mass to pressure, volume, and temperature. "Chemical Moles" helps students see the usefulness of balanced equations and molar mass. "Endothermic and Exothermic Reactions" is a high-interest experiment that explains the role of activation energy in chemical reactions that impact our daily lives.

The use of models and manipulatives is a good way to gain understanding of abstract ideas. In "Lewis Structures" students use models to gain a better understanding of the roles of valence electrons in the formation of chemical bonds. "Ozone Depletion" addresses the causes of thinning of ozone layer and enables students to understand the damaging roles of CFCs using models of their own design.

Two of the experiments in *Chemistry Science Experiments* are inquiries, experiments in which students are given a problem and asked to write a hypothesis, design and conduct an experiment, and draw conclusions. Inquiry experiments also serve as differentiation tools for teachers who want to fine tune their instruction to individual students. Experiments that provide students with the opportunities to carry out inquiries include "The Rate of Rusting" and "Solutes Affect the Boiling Point of Water." Students are asked to design experiments in "The Rate of Rusting" to understand what happens in redox reactions. In "Solutes Affect the Boiling Point of Water," students are provided with basic information on the effects of dissolved molecules on boiling, then told to carry out an experiment of their own design.

Walker and Wood focused on applied chemistry, the utilization of the principles of chemistry for practical purposes, in this book in the hope that students would relate to the experiments and realize that all of us are chemists who work with chemical reactions on a daily basis. By guiding learners through these experiments, teachers can help students come to the realization that chemistry is the discipline that is most relevant to our lives because it is the study of the world in which we live. Once students make that connection, they are on their way to being life-long learners of science.

Safety Precautions

REVIEW BEFORE STARTING ANY EXPERIMENT

Each experiment includes special safety precautions that are relevant to that particular project. These do not include all the basic safety precautions that are necessary whenever you are working on a scientific experiment. For this reason, it is absolutely necessary that you read and remain mindful of the General Safety Precautions that follow. Experimental science can be dangerous and good laboratory procedure always includes following basic safety rules. Things can happen quickly while you are performing an experiment—for example, materials can spill, break, or even catch on fire. There will not be time after the fact to protect yourself. Always prepare for unexpected dangers by following the basic safety guidelines during the entire experiment, whether or not something seems dangerous to you at a given moment.

We have been quite sparing in prescribing safety precautions for the individual experiments. For one reason, we want you to take very seriously the safety precautions that are printed in this book. If you see it written here, you can be sure that it is here because it is absolutely critical.

Read the safety precautions here and at the beginning of each experiment before performing each lab activity. It is difficult to remember a long set of general rules. By rereading these general precautions every time you set up an experiment, you will be reminding yourself that lab safety is critically important. In addition, use your good judgment and pay close attention when performing potentially dangerous procedures. Just because the book does not say "Be careful with hot liquids" or "Don't cut yourself with a knife" does not mean that you can be careless when boiling water or using a knife to punch holes in plastic bottles. Notes in the text are special precautions to which you must pay special attention.

GENERAL SAFETY PRECAUTIONS

Accidents can be caused by carelessness, haste, or insufficient knowledge. By practicing safety procedures and being alert while conducting experiments, you can avoid taking an unnecessary risk. Be sure to check the individual experiments in this book for additional safety regulations and adult supervision requirements. If you will be working in a laboratory, do not work alone. When you are working off site, keep in groups with a minimum of three students per group, and follow school rules and state legal requirements for the number of supervisors required. Ask an adult supervisor with basic training in first aid to carry a small first-aid kit. Make sure everyone knows where this person will be during the experiment.

PREPARING

- Clear all surfaces before beginning experiments.
- Read the entire experiment before you start.
- Know the hazards of the experiments and anticipate dangers.

PROTECTING YOURSELF

- Follow the directions step by step.
- Perform only one experiment at a time.
- Locate exits, fire blanket and extinguisher, master gas and electricity shut-offs, eyewash, and first-aid kit.
- Make sure there is adequate ventilation.
- Do not participate in horseplay.
- Do not wear open-toed shoes.
- Keep floor and workspace neat, clean, and dry.
- Clean up spills immediately.
- If glassware breaks, do not clean it up by yourself; ask for teacher assistance.
- Tie back long hair.
- Never eat, drink, or smoke in the laboratory or workspace.
- Do not eat or drink any substances tested unless expressly permitted to do so by a knowledgeable adult.

USING EQUIPMENT WITH CARE

- Set up apparatus far from the edge of the desk.
- Use knives or other sharp, pointed instruments with care.

- Pull plugs, not cords, when removing electrical plugs.
- Clean glassware before and after use.
- Check glassware for scratches, cracks, and sharp edges.
- Let your teacher know about broken glassware immediately.
- Do not use reflected sunlight to illuminate your microscope.
- Do not touch metal conductors.
- Take care when working with any form of electricity.
- Use alcohol-filled thermometers, not mercury-filled thermometers.

USING CHEMICALS

- Never taste or inhale chemicals.
- Label all bottles and apparatus containing chemicals.
- Read labels carefully.
- Avoid chemical contact with skin and eyes (wear safety glasses or goggles, lab apron, and gloves).
- Do not touch chemical solutions.
- Wash hands before and after using solutions.
- Wipe up spills thoroughly.

HEATING SUBSTANCES

- Wear safety glasses or goggles, apron, and gloves when heating materials.
- Keep your face away from test tubes and beakers.
- When heating substances in a test tube, avoid pointing the top of the test tube toward other people.
- Use test tubes, beakers, and other glassware made of Pyrex™ glass.
- Never leave apparatus unattended.
- Use safety tongs and heat-resistant gloves.
- If your laboratory does not have heatproof workbenches, put your Bunsen burner on a heatproof mat before lighting it.
- Take care when lighting your Bunsen burner; light it with the airhole closed and use a Bunsen burner lighter rather than wooden matches.

- Turn off hot plates, Bunsen burners, and gas when you are done.
- Keep flammable substances away from flames and other sources of heat.
- Have a fire extinguisher on hand.

FINISHING UP

- Thoroughly clean your work area and any glassware used.
- Wash your hands.
- Be careful not to return chemicals or contaminated reagents to the wrong containers.
- Do not dispose of materials in the sink unless instructed to do so.
- Clean up all residues and put in proper containers for disposal.
- Dispose of all chemicals according to all local, state, and federal laws.

BE SAFETY CONSCIOUS AT ALL TIMES!

1. The Smell of an Ester

Topic

Esters prepared in the classroom can be identified by their characteristic odors.

Introduction

An *ester* is a type of organic chemical that produces distinctive odors. Many fruits, vegetables, and animal fats contain esters. Because these chemicals have pleasant odors, some are synthetically produced in order to create artificial scents and flavorings. An ester is derived from the combination of a *carboxylic acid* and an alcohol, two organic compounds. Carboxylic acids contain a –COOH group, and alcohols contain an –OH group. These functional groups react and combine through *dehydration synthesis*, a chemical reaction in which the –OH from the alcohol and the –H from the carboxylic acid are removed to form a water molecule, permitting the two compounds to chemically combine. The general formula for an ester is RCOOR, shown in Figure 1.

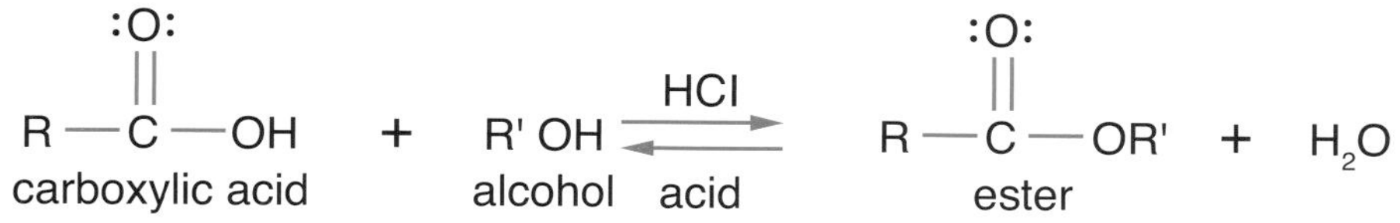

Figure 1

An ester is formed by the combination of a carboxylic acid and an alcohol.

The characteristics of esters vary depending on the R-groups that are attached to the alcohol and the acid functional groups. By varying the combination of carboxylic acids and alcohol, a variety of compounds can be created. Some common esters are listed on Data Table 1. The most often used process of creating esters is known as Fischer esterification. In this experiment, you will use Fisher esterification to create a variety of esters from different combinations of acids and alcohols and compare their odors.

Data Table 1

Carboxylic Acid	Alcohol	Ester Name	Scent
Butyric Acid	Methanol	Methyl butyrate	Pineapple or apple
Benzanoic Acid	Methanol	Methyl benzoate	Fruity
Trans-cinnamic Acid	Methanol	Methyl cinnamate	Strawberry
Trans-cinnamic Acid	Ethanol	Ethyl cinnamate	Cinnamon
Formic Acid	Ethanol	Ethyl formate	Rum
Salicylic Acid	Ethanol	Ethyl salcylate	Oil of Wintergreen
Heptanoic Acid	Ethanol	Ethyl heptanoate	Grape
Formic Acid	Isobutanol	Isobutyl formate	Raspberry
Butyric Acid	Butanol	Butyl butyrate	Pineapple
Acetic Acid	Pentanol	Pentyl acetate	Banana
Butyric Acid	Pentanol	Pentyl butyrate	Pear or apricot
Acetic Acid	Octanol	Octyl acetate	Fruity orange

Time Required

30 minutes

Materials

For the class:

- beakers containing about 100 milliliters (ml) of concentrated solution or 50 grams (g) of solid for the following acids:

- ✔ glacial acetic acid
- ✔ benzanoic acid (solid)
- ✔ butryic acid
- ✔ formic acid
- ✔ heptanoic acid
- ✔ trans-cinnamic acid (solid)
- beakers containing about 100 ml of the following concentrated alcohols:
  - ✔ methanol
  - ✔ ethanol
  - ✔ isobutanol
  - ✔ butanol
  - ✔ pentanol
  - ✔ octanol
- plastic 1-ml measuring pipettes (one for each solution)
- microspatulas (one for each solid reagent)
- dropper bottle of 18 Molar (M) sulfuric acid (under a fume hood)
- 5 percent solution of baking soda in water

For each group:

- hot plate
- large (400 to 600 ml) beaker
- distilled water
- 4 large test tubes
- 4 test-tube stoppers with a single hole bored through
- test-tube rack
- 4 stirring rods
- thermometer
- test-tube clamp
- chemistry book or access to the Internet
- goggles (one pair for each student)

⊶   hot mitts

⊶   science notebook

Safety Note   Goggles must be worn at all times during this experiment. Use extreme caution when working with strong acids and flammable alcohols. The lab should be completed in a well-ventilated area. Use a fume hood for the entire experiment if possible. Store the concentrated acids under the fume hood. Be cautious when heating chemicals, as they may splatter and heating may cause glassware to shatter. Use hot mitts when handling hot objects. Please review and follow the safety guidelines at the beginning of this volume.

Procedure

1. Examine Data Table 1 which lists esters, their ingredients, and their scents. Select four esters that you would like to create in this experiment.

2. Copy Data Table 2 in your science notebook. On the data table, record the esters you plan to make. Also write down the acid and alcohol that you will use for each ester.

3. Fill a large beaker about half full of water. Place the beaker on a hot plate and bring the water to a temperature between 176 to 194 degrees Fahrenheit (°F) (80 to 90 degrees Celsius [°C]). Maintain this temperature throughout the lab. Do not allow the water to reach the boiling point.

4. Label four test tubes 1 through 4. These numbers will correspond with the esters, acids, and alcohols you recorded on Data Table 2.

5. Add 1 ml of the appropriate acid to test tube 1. Be sure to avoid mixing up the pipettes in the reagent beakers to prevent cross contamination. (If the acids are in the solid form, add 1 microspatula scoop.)

6. Add 1 ml of the appropriate alcohol to the same test tube. (Be sure not to mix up the pipettes in the reagent beakers.)

7. While holding the test tube about 12 inches (in.) (30.5 centimeters [cm]) from your face, gently wave your hand over the top of each test tube toward your nose until you can smell the ester (see Figure 2). (Do not place your nose directly above the test tube.) Describe the scent in your science notebook.

8. Add 3 to 4 drops of concentrated sulfuric acid to the test tube and stir gently.

9. Stopper the test tube and place in the test-tube rack.

Figure 2

To smell the substance in a test tube, wave your hand over the tube toward your nose.

10. Repeat steps 5 through 10 with test tubes 2, 3, and 4, using the acids and alcohols listed on Data Table 2.

11. Place all four test tubes in the hot water bath for about 5 minutes (min).

12. After 5 min, remove the test tubes from the hot water and allow them to cool for 1 to 2 min in the test tube rack.

13. Remove the stoppers and add 8 to 10 drops of 5 percent baking soda solution to each test tube to react with the excess acid and make the scent of the esters more evident.

14. While holding the test tube about 12 in. (30.5 cm) from your face, gently wave the scent of each test tube toward your nose until you can smell the ester. (Do not place your nose directly above the test tube.)

15. Record the scent of each ester in Data Table 2.

Analysis

1. Research the four esters that you chose to create in this lab. Draw their chemical structures in your science notebook.

2. How were the scents of the *reagents* (acids and alcohols) different from the scents of the *products* (esters) in this lab?

3. Compare the observed scent for each of the four esters you created to the scents that are described on Data Table 1. Were your actual results the same as the expected results? If not, why do you think the scent was different?

Data Table 2				
Test tube	Ester	Carboxylic acid	Alcohol	Observed scent
1				
2				
3				
4				

4. How do you think the results of this lab would have differed if the test tubes were not heated? If sulfuric acid were not added?
5. Esters occur naturally, yet are commonly artificially created through the lab processes of esterification. In what industries would this process be beneficial?

What's Going On?

The chemical reaction to produce esters is easily reversible. This means that under normal conditions, there are equal amounts of ester product and reagents, carboxylic acid and alcohol. Since the reagents have an odor that is very different from the scent of the ester that they produce, the combined odor would not be as pleasant as the desired scent of the ester alone.

The Fischer esterification process used in this lab is a good way to produce esters because it increases the yield to nearly 95 percent. In order to obtain a high yield of ester product, a strong acid, such as sulfuric acid, is used to *catalyze* the reaction. Sulfuric acid is a strong dehydrating agent, which removes water from the reaction and helps to drive the reaction toward the production of more ester product formed by dehydration synthesis. Additionally, the reaction occurs best when heated. As the solution is warmed, water evaporates, which also helps to increase the ester production.

Connections

Esters are only one type of organic chemical that can be detected by senses. Animals use chemical signals called *pheromones* to communicate and trigger responses in others within their species. Pheromones are a type of organic compound, generally composed of different combinations of ring structures, esters, and hydrocarbons. These specialized chemicals are used for a variety of purposes, including attracting mates, sending warnings to others, marking trails to food sources, and calling others to aggregate in a certain area.

The structure of a pheromone can vary greatly depending on the species and the specific response that it triggers, but most are fairly small molecules so that they can be easily produced by glands and transmitted great distances through the air. Pheromones are commonly synthesized artificially as attractants or repellants that can be used as a method of pest control.

Figure 3

A pheromone is used to lure boll weevils into traps like this one.

Want to Know More?

See appendix for Our Findings.

Further Reading

Clark, Jim. "Esters Menu," 2009. ChemGuide. Available online. URL: http://www.chemguide.co.uk/organicprops/esters/background.html#top. Accessed July 17, 2010. Clark explains the chemistry of esters and shows their chemical formulas.

Knight, A. R. Hilton, P. Van Buskirk, and D. Light. "Using pear ester to monitor codling moth in sex pheromone treated orchards," February 2006. Available online: URL: http://extension.oregonstate.edu/catalog/pdf/em/em8904.pdf. Accessed July 17, 2010. This article explains a practical application of synthetic esters in agriculture.

"Organic Chemistry," 2010. Vision Learning. Available online. URL: http://www.visionlearning.com/library/module_viewer.php?mid=60. Accessed July 17, 2010. This Web site provides a good introduction to basic organic chemistry, including functional groups.

2. The Chemistry of Toothpaste

Topic

The chemical qualities of several brands of toothpaste can be tested to compare the effectiveness of the products.

Introduction

Toothpaste has been around since ancient Egyptian times. The first toothpastes, made from a combination of flowers, salt, and spices, were scrubbed on the teeth with a cloth. Toothpastes and powders were also known in ancient China and India where they were predominantly made of abrasive substances, such as crushed bones or shells. However, these products did not become widely used until the 19th century when homemade mixtures of chalk, soap, and salt or abrasive substances found their ways into homes. Late in the century, toothpastes made from baking soda and peroxide were being commercially produced. In 1914, manufacturers started adding *fluoride* to these products because of fluoride's cavity-preventing properties. Adding fluoride to toothpastes became widespread when fluoridation was approved by the American Dental Association in the 1950s.

Toothpastes have evolved since then. Today, there are countless varieties containing ingredients that prevent cavities, reduce tartar, whiten teeth, reduce sensitivity, and freshen breath. Toothpastes come in many flavors, colors, and textures as seen in Figure 1. Regardless of the variety, most products include three basic ingredients: an abrasive agent, a source of sodium, and a type of detergent or foaming substance. In this experiment, you will choose five different varieties of toothpaste and compare their chemical properties.

 **Time Required**

30 minutes

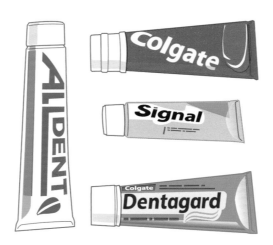

Figure 1

Toothpastes are available in a variety of formulations.

Materials

- 5 different brands or varieties (such as whitening, tartar control, sensitive, anticavity, plaque preventing, and breath freshening) of toothpaste
- pH paper
- fluoride test strips
- distilled water (about 10 milliliter [ml])
- aluminum foil
- test tubes (about 5 per group)
- test-tube rack
- Parafilm™ or test-tube stoppers
- 10-ml graduated cylinder
- spatulas
- cotton swabs (at least 5 per group)
- ruler
- masking tape
- permanent marker
- science notebook

| Safety Note | Please review and follow the safety guidelines at the beginning of this volume. |

Procedure

1. Answer Analysis questions 1 and 2.

2. Label five test tubes 1 through 5. Write the names of the five types of toothpaste you will be testing on Data Table 1; the numbers on the data table and the test tubes will correlate with the type of toothpaste to be tested.

3. Place 1 to 2 ml of toothpaste into each of the designated test tubes and place the tubes into a test-tube rack. Make notes on the appearance and texture of each toothpaste on the data table.

4. Test the pH of toothpaste 1 by placing a strip of pH paper into the test tube (or scooping a small amount out of the tube with a spatula and testing the small sample). Compare the color of the strip to the indicator card and record the pH of the solution on the data table (see Figure 2). Repeat with samples 2 through 5.

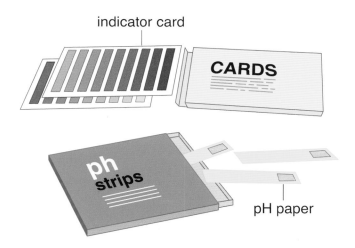

Figure 2

Determine the pH of the substance tested by comparing the color of the pH paper to the indicator card.

5. Test the fluoride content of toothpaste 1 by placing a fluoride test strip into the test tube or by testing a small amount on a spatula. Compare the test strip to the indicator card. Record the fluoride content on the data table. Repeat with samples 2 through 5.

6. To test the abrasiveness of each toothpaste, spread a piece of aluminum foil onto a flat surface (shiny side up) and tape it down. Using a ruler and permanent marker, draw five 1-inch (in.) by 1-in. (2.5-centimeters [cm] by 2.5-cm) boxes on the foil. Label the boxes 1 through 5.

7. Test the abrasiveness of toothpaste 1 by dipping a cotton swab into the test tube and then rubbing the swab of toothpaste back and forth 10 times across the entire length of box 1 on the aluminum foil. Wipe the toothpaste from the foil with a tissue or soft cloth. Repeat with samples 2 through 5.

8. Observe the damage to the foil in boxes 1 through 5. Rank the abrasiveness of each toothpaste on a scale of 1 to 10 (1 being the most abrasive and causing a lot of damage to the foil, and 10 being the least abrasive with no damage to the foil). Record abrasiveness of each toothpaste on the data table.

9. To test the foaming action of toothpaste 1, measure 2 ml of distilled water in a graduated cylinder. Add to test tube 1 and use a stopper or Parafilm™ to close the top. Shake vigorously for 30 seconds. Repeat with samples 2 through 5.

10. Rank the foaming action of each sample on a scale from 1 to 10 (when 1 equals no foam and 10 equals very foamy). Record foaming action on the data table.

11. Clean out all tubes and answer Analysis questions 3 through 6.

Data Table						
Tube	Toothpaste	Appearance	pH	Fluoride	Abrasiveness	Foaming
1						
2						
3						
4						
5						

Analysis

1. Read the labels of the five different toothpastes and list any differences in ingredients among toothpastes.

2. Which toothpaste do you think will be the most acidic? Basic? Have the most fluoride? Be the most abrasive? Foam the most? Explain why you made each of these predictions.

3. Did your experimental results agree with your predictions? Why or why not?

4. Compare the results from this test with the list of different ingredients in each type of toothpaste. How do you think these ingredients influence the properties of different varieties of toothpaste?

5. Were all of your toothpaste samples the same brand? If not, were there any differences between two similar varieties of toothpaste with different brand names?

6. Based on your results from this experiment, do the ingredients in toothpaste make a difference in their chemical properties? Explain your answer.

What's Going On?

Today's toothpastes have many different ingredients and varieties. Most toothpastes are somewhat basic because of the baking soda and detergents present in them. However, the pH of toothpastes can vary. Additives such as flavoring and whitening agents like hydrogen peroxide can cause the pH to drop, while antibacterial agents, baking soda, and detergents can cause the pH to increase. Most toothpastes today use sodium fluoride as a source of fluoride ions, although some use sodium monophosphate instead. The amount of fluoride in toothpastes is regulated because it can be toxic in large amounts, but the concentration generally falls into the 1,000- to 1,450-parts-per-million range. Toothpastes usually contain some type of detergent or surfactant such as sodium lauryl sulfate or ammonium lauryl sulfate that acts as a foaming agent and helps to remove debris from the teeth. Additionally, they may contain antibacterial additives such as triclosan or zinc to destroy bacteria in the mouth. The abrasive agents in toothpastes are usually composed of hydrated silica, silicon dioxide, or titanium dioxide.

Toothpastes that are specialized for certain purposes contain special additives that may change their chemical properties. Tartar control toothpastes contain substances such as tetrasodium pyrophosphate to prevent the build up of tartar. Toothpastes for sensitive teeth generally contain a desensitizing agent such as strontium chloride, potassium nitrate, or potassium citrate. Whitening toothpastes contain hydrogen peroxide or sodium carbonate peroxide to remove stains from the teeth.

Connections

In the early 20th century, scientists found that fluoride had properties that would prevent tooth decay. This discovery was made based on a study of children in rural areas of Colorado who had mysterious brown stains on their teeth but had an amazingly low incidence of cavities. Upon researching and testing for the cause of the problem, it was concluded that the brown stains and the lack of tooth decay were due to the presence of fluoride ions in their drinking water. Scientists concluded that while large amounts of fluoride could cause stains on the teeth or even poisoning, small doses of fluoride, about 1 gram (g) per liter (L), added to drinking water could help to prevent cavities. Fluoride can protect teeth from decay by strengthening the enamel and preventing acid erosion of teeth (Figure 3).

In the 1950s many communities began fluoridating municipal water sources in order to reduce the number of cavities in the community. This process has been fairly controversial because fluoride can have harmful effects if not monitored properly. Regardless of the controversy associated with this practice, around 69 percent of Americans were receiving fluoridated water in their homes in 2006. The Centers for Disease Control hopes to increase that number to 75 percent by the end of 2010.

Want to Know More?

See appendix for Our Findings.

Further Reading

"Chemistry in a Tube of Toothpaste," 2010. HowStuffWorks. Available online. URL: http://science.howstuffworks.com/chemistry-in-a-tube-of-toothpaste-info.htm. Accessed July 17, 2010. The history of toothpaste and the chemical effects of various ingredients are explained in this article.

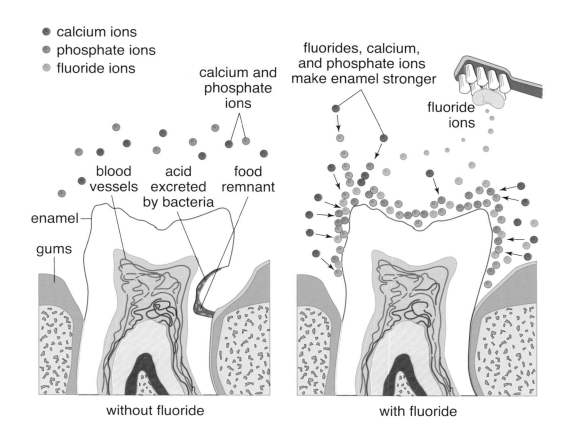

calcium ions
phosphate ions
fluoride ions

calcium and phosphate ions

fluorides, calcium, and phosphate ions make enamel stronger

fluoride ions

blood vessels   acid excreted by bacteria   food remnant

enamel

gums

without fluoride

with fluoride

Figure 3

Fluoride ions can bind to enamel, the hard outer layer of teeth, and make it stronger.

"Fluoride Facts," 2010. American Dental Hygienists' Association. Available online. URL: http://www.adha.org/oralhealth/fluoride_facts.htm. Accessed July 17, 2010. This easy-to-read Web page explains the benefits of fluoride treatment on teeth.

Stevenson, Seth. "Paste Test," *Slate*, October 7, 1998. Available online. URL: http://www.slate.com/id/3604/. Accessed July 17, 2010. Stevenson explains the purposes of various chemicals used in toothpastes in this article.

3. Water Softeners

Topic

The qualities of water softened by two different techniques can be compared.

Introduction

Many homes experience problems with *hard water*, water that contains calcium or magnesium ions that interfere with the ability of soap to work properly. Hard water can clog and eventually ruin pipes (Figure 1) and can cause stains and buildup on sinks, bathtubs, and toilets within the home. Unlike hard water, *soft water* contains only sodium ions, which do not interfere with soap's ability to create suds. There are many different types of water softening devices that are commonly used in homes that experience problems with hard water.

Figure 1

Ions in hard water can build up inside of pipes

In some cases, water can be softened by *distillation*, a process that involves boiling water, capturing the vapor, then condensing it back into a liquid. Hard water can also be softened by treatment with *lime* and *soda ash,* followed by filtration to remove the precipitates that were formed. Another way to remove calcium and magnesium ions is by replacing them with sodium by filteration through an *ion exchange resin*. In this experiment, you will choose two methods of water softening, develop a procedure to test both methods, and compare their effectiveness.

Time Required

45 minutes

Materials

- distilled water (about 5 milliliters [ml])
- access to running water
- hard water (distilled water treated with 15 ml (1 tablespoon [tbsp]) Epsom salt per 1.06 quarts [qt] [1 liter (L)])
- dish washing liquid (not detergent used in a dishwasher)
- hot plate or Bunsen burner with ring stand, iron ring, and wire gauze
- goggles
- hot mitts
- ring stand with clamp
- 2 250 ml beakers
- 2 600 ml beakers
- graduated cylinder
- thermometer
- florence flask
- condenser tube for distillation
- 2 hoses for the distillation condenser (each about 3 feet (ft) [about 1 meter (m)] long)
- 2-hole stopper
- 1-hole stopper
- 3 test tubes with stoppers
- Parafilm™
- plastic pipettes

➥ lime-soda ash mixture (equal parts of calcium hydroxide and sodium bicarbonate) (about 0.5 cups [c]) (118 ml)

➥ ion exchange resin beads (about 0.4 c [100 ml])

➥ large plastic funnel

➥ electronic balance

➥ filtration flask with vacuum hose

➥ vacuum pump

➥ filter paper

➥ access to the Internet or a chemistry textbook

➥ science notebook

Safety Note **Goggles must be worn at all times during this experiment. Use extreme caution with the strong bases used in this experiment. Be careful when heating glassware or when using water near electricity sources. Use hot mitts to handle hot objects. Do not drink the water used in this experiment. Please review and follow the safety guidelines at the beginning of this volume.**

Procedure

1. Test distilled water for soap foaming action. To do so, pour 2 ml of water into a test tube and add 1 to 2 drops of dish washing liquid with a pipette. Cover with a stopper or Parafilm™ and shake vigorously for 10 seconds. Record your observations on the data table.

2. Repeat the foaming action test with 2 ml of hard water. Record your observations on the data table.

3. Described below are three techniques used for water softening: distillation, lime-soda ash treatment, and ion exchange resin treatment. Read all three methods, then select two to try in this experiment.

4. Soften two samples of water, using the two techniques you selected.

   A. Distillation

   1. Set up the distillation apparatus as shown in Figure 2. Attach a water input hose to one valve on the condenser and attach a water output hose to the other. Place a beaker below the condenser to collect the distilled water.

2. Place 200 ml of hard water in the florence flask, then light the Bunsen burner. If you are using a hot plate instead of a Bunsen burner, turn it on.

3. Heat the water in the flask until it boils and begins to evaporate. Turn down the Bunsen burner or hot plate so that you can continue to boil the water gently until about 0.2 inches (about 0.5 centimeters [cm]) of water remains in the bottom of the flask. When you are finished boiling water, turn off the heat source.

4. After the condenser stops dripping, remove the beaker from below the apparatus. Set aside the beaker of water for procedure step 5.

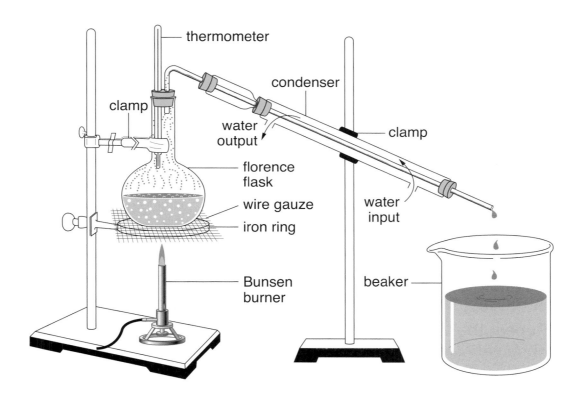

Figure 2

Distillation equipment setup

B. Lime/Soda Ash Treatment

1. Add 5 to 8 grams (g) of lime-soda ash mixture to a beaker containing 200 ml of hard water.

2. Stir vigorously for 30 seconds.

3. Allow the mixture to settle while you set up a vacuum filtration flask by placing the filtration funnel in the flask and connecting a hose to the vacuum valve. Place a piece of filter paper in the top of the funnel.

4. Pour the water/lime-soda ash mixture slowly into the filtration apparatus. Turn on the vacuum to begin the filtration process.

5. When filtration is complete, turn off the vacuum and remove the beaker from below the apparatus. Set aside the beaker of water for procedure step 5.

C. Ion Exchange Resin Treatment

1. Place a piece of filter paper in the top of a funnel and fill the funnel with ion exchange resin beads.

2. Place the funnel over a large beaker.

3. Measure 200 ml of hard water and pour it slowly into the funnel containing resin beads.

4. Allow the water to filter through the resin and collect the softened water from the large beaker. Set aside the beaker of water for procedure step 5.

5. Measure 2 ml of the softened water from each procedure and repeat the foaming action test from step 1. Record your observations on the data table.

6. Rank all four samples tested—those tested in step 1 and those tested in step 5—in order of foaming action from 1 to 4, with the sample foaming least as 1, and the sample foaming most as 4.

Data Table				
Sample	**Pure water**	**Hard water**	**Treatment 1** _____	**Treatment 2** _____
Observations				
Foam rating				

Analysis

1. Describe the two methods of water softening you used in this experiment. Why did you choose these methods?

2. Which of the samples tested in this lab foamed the most? The least? Explain your results.

3. Why does soap not lather in hard water? What is different about softened water that enables soap to foam?

4. On the Internet or in chemistry books, research the prevalence of hard water. What causes water to "harden"?

5. Certain areas of the United States experience hard water more than others. How do environmental and geological factors influence the production of hard water?

6. What are some of the disadvantages of using water softeners?

What's Going On?

Hard water contains *ions* such as calcium and magnesium that prevent soap from lathering as much as in soft water. These ions also tend to create an insoluble substance that can cause stains on tubs and sinks and create buildup in pipes, which can eventually destroy them. Hard water is more of a problem in certain areas than others because of the minerals present in the *groundwater* in that area (See Figure 3). In order to soften water, many homes in areas that have a high occurrence of hard water use a variety of treatments and filtration processes. The process of distillation is sometimes effective in removing ions and impurities from water. This process allows water to evaporate and then condense back into a purified liquid. After water is boiled, the water vapor is cooled back into a liquid and collected. This process is not generally as effective as *reverse osmosis*, a much more expensive filtering alternative. In reverse osmosis, water is pressurized against a membrane, forcing water molecules through the membrane and leaving ions behind. Reverse osmosis filters are commonly used in homes to soften water, but since the pumps are large and expensive, the process was not used in this experiment.

Ion replacement treatments are much more cost effective than reverse osmosis and are more effective at removing calcium and magnesium than distillation. Treatment with lime and soda ash is effective at replacing calcium and magnesium ions with sodium ions, but the resulting liquid must be filtered very well and treated with additional chemicals to purify it for drinking. Filters that contain beads of ion replacement resin are just as effective as lime and soda ash. However, the resin sometimes makes water taste salty and can cause problems for individuals with *high blood pressure*.

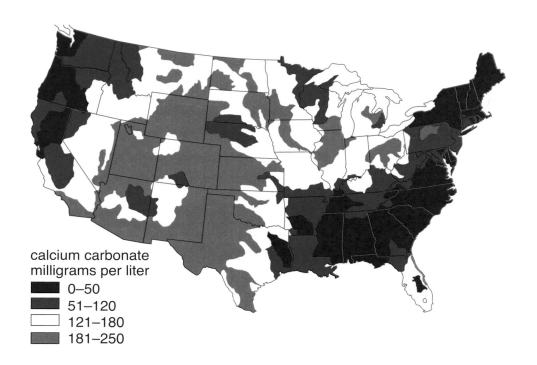

Figure 3

Occurrence of hard water in the continental United States. On this map, water hardness is indicated by the amount of calcium carbonate in milligrams per liter.

Connections

Hard water is generally considered to be undesirable because of the buildup that it can cause in pipes, sinks, showers, and bathtubs and because it causes soap not to lather as well. However, the minerals that occur naturally in groundwater have many health benefits. Our bodies require certain minerals in order to work properly, and many of those occur naturally in the water that we drink. Minerals often work as cofactors that help enzymes to work and they are important in many other regular cell processes. Not only do minerals have health benefits, but they also give water a desirable taste. Many bottled water companies add minerals back to water in order to replenish the "natural" taste.

Want to Know More?

See appendix for Our Findings.

Further Reading

"Hard Water." Wilkes University Center for Environmental Quality Environmental Engineering and Earth Sciences. Available online. URL: http://www.water-research.net/hardness.htm. Accessed July 17, 2010. This Web site explains sources of hard water, indications of hard water, and health concerns.

Helmenstine, Anne Marie. "Chemistry of Hard and Soft Water," Available online. URL: http://www.lifesourcewater.com/water-knowledge/hard-soft-water.html. Accessed July 17, 2010. In this article, Helmenstine provides a simple explanation of the difference between hard and soft water and discusses some hard water problems.

"How Does a Water Softener Work?" 2010. HowStuffWorks. Available online. URL: http://home.howstuffworks.com/question99.htm. Accessed July 17, 2010. This article explains some techniques of water softening and includes a video demonstrating the installation of a water softening device.

4. Lewis Structures

Topic

Lewis structures can be used to predict bonding capabilities of molecules.

Introduction

An atom has a tiny but dense nucleus that is composed of positively charged protons and neutral neutrons. The nucleus is surrounded by negatively charged electrons that orbit in paths known as *orbitals*. Atoms are stable when their outermost orbitals are full of electrons. For all elements other than hydrogen and helium (which have only one and two electrons respectively), the outer shell is considered to be full when it contains eight electrons, an *octet*. These outer shell electrons are known as *valence electrons*. A Lewis dot structure, which is a diagram that represents an atom, shows the valence electrons. In this type of diagram, electrons are represented by dots that surround the element symbol. Dots are positioned on each side of the symbol (top, bottom, left, and right). Figure 1 shows Lewis dot structures for several elements.

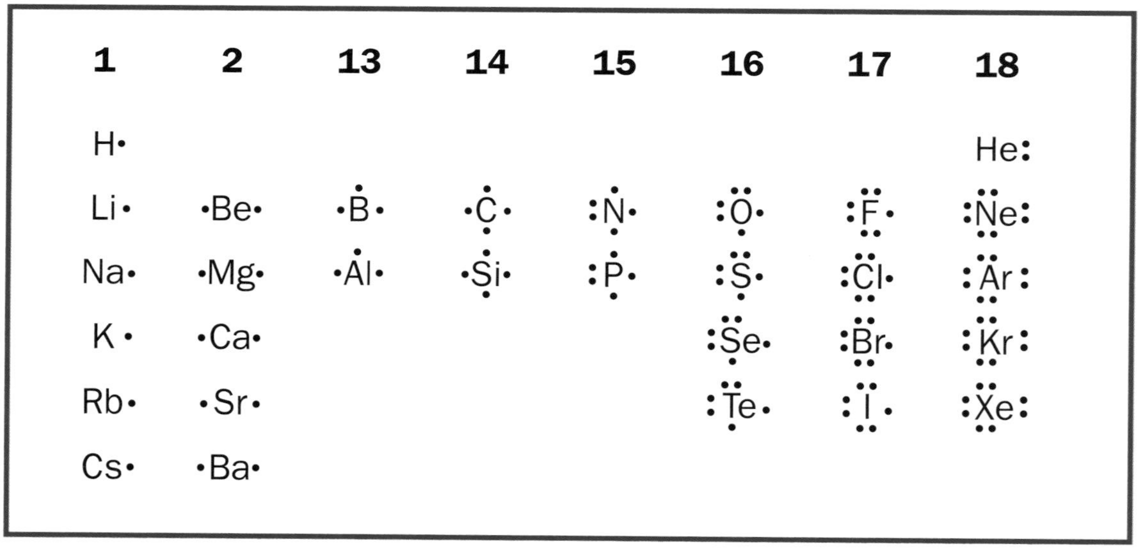

1	2	13	14	15	16	17	18
H•							He:
Li•	•Be•	•Ḃ•	•Ċ•	:Ṅ•	:Ö•	:F̈•	:N̈e:
Na•	•Mg•	•Al•	•Si•	:Ṗ•	:S̈•	:C̈l•	:Är:
K•	•Ca•				:Se•	:Br•	:Kr:
Rb•	•Sr•				:Te•	:Ï•	:Xe:
Cs•	•Ba•						

Figure 1

**Lewis dot structures for elements in groups 1 and 2
and 13 through 18 of the periodic table.**

Atoms will bond with other atoms until they have eight valence electrons, which gives them stability. In a *covalent bond*, two *nonmetal* atoms share electrons to become stable. Each shared pair of electrons creates a bond between the two elements. *Ionic bonds* occur between *metals* and nonmetals. In an ionic bond, one element (a metal) loses electrons and becomes positively charged. Another element (a nonmetal) gains electrons and becomes negatively charged. The opposite charges between elements cause an attraction that creates an ionic bond. In this activity, you will build Lewis dot structures and demonstrate the different types of bonding using colored candies as electrons.

Time Required

30 minutes

Materials

- plastic cup containing about 30 M&Ms™ (or other small colorful candies)
- periodic table of elements (see page 175)
- 3 x 5 index cards (about 40)
- science notebook

Safety Note   Please review and follow the safety guidelines at the beginning of this volume.

Procedure

1. Create Lewis dot representations for the elements in the compound NH_3. To do so:

    a. Write the symbol N in the center of one index card.

    b. In the center of three other cards, write the symbol H.

    c. Look at the periodic table and compare it to Figure 2, which shows the number of valence electrons for elements in groups 1 and 2 and 13 through 18. Determine how many valence electrons are found in nitrogen (N). You will see that N has five valence electrons.

   d. To represent these valence electrons, arrange 5 candies on the index card around the N in the pattern shown in Figure 3.

   e. Refer to the periodic table to see that each hydrogen atom has one valence electron.

   f. Place one candy on each index card beside each H.

   g. Determine whether NH_3 is an ionic or covalent compound. (Remember, atoms form ionic bonds if they are both nonmetals; they form covalent bonds if one is a metal and the other a nonmetal. You can determine whether an element is a metal or nonmetal by its position on the periodic table.) Nitrogen is a metal and hydrogen is a nonmetal, so these two elements form a covalent compound. Write a C in the corner of the N card to represent covalent.

   h. Position the three H cards around the N card. Arrange the candies so that N shares electrons with the three Hs. Draw circles around the shared pairs. Keep in mind that when atoms share electrons, each atom counts those electrons (see Figure 4).

   i. Sketch the Lewis dot structures for NH_3 on Data Table 1.

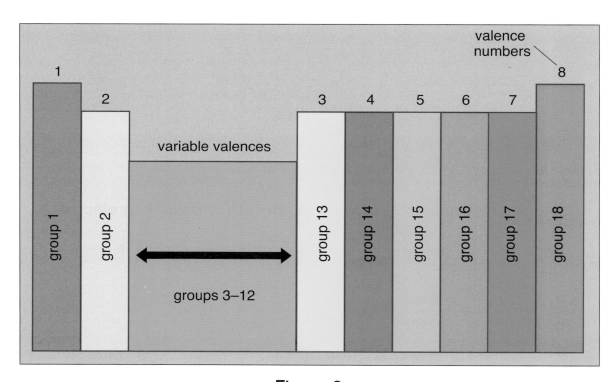

Figure 2

Valence electrons for elements in groups 1 and 2 and 13 through 18 of the periodic table.

Figure 3

Nitrogen has five valence electrons, represented by black dots

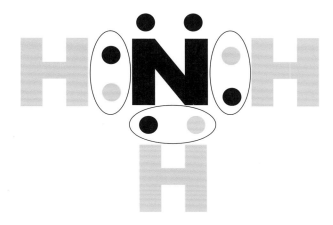

Figure 4

Each hydrogen atom has one valence electron, represented by a yellow dot. Nitrogen shares electrons with three hydrogen atoms. Shared electrons are circled. This arrangement provides nitrogen with eight valence electrons and each hydrogen with two valence electrons.

2. Repeat step 1 for the other compounds listed on page 28. As you arrange candies, use the same color for one element. For example, use only red candies for lithium and green for bromine. Remember that each atom, with the exception of hydrogen and helium, should have eight candies around it once it has formed a compound. Also remember that if an element has a subscript, you will have to create that number of cards with the symbol on each. Be sure to keep together the cards for elements that are in a compound. Write a C on the cards of elements in covalent compounds and draw those compounds on Data Table 1. Label ionic compounds with an I and draw them on Data Table 2.

NH_3	$LiBr$	CH_4	H_2O
$CaCl_2$	CO_2	PCl_3	Na_2O
N_2	H_2	KI	SrF_2

Data Table 1	
Covalent compounds	**Lewis structures**
NH_3	

Data Table 2	
Ionic compounds	**Lewis structures**

Analysis

1. List three differences between ionic and covalent compounds.
2. Covalent bonds are much stronger than ionic ones. Based on the Lewis structures you created, why do you think this is?
3. Metals do not participate in covalent bonds. Explain why.
4. What determines whether an atom forms a positive or negative charge in an ionic bond?
5. Could you have a compound with the formula HS_3? Why or why not?

What's Going On?

The valence, or outer shell electrons, of an atom determine how they participate in reactions with one another. Atoms bond to gain stability by having a full valence shell. Atoms on the left side of the periodic table are metals. These atoms generally have three or fewer electrons in their outermost shell, so they tend to donate their electrons. A metal can lose its valence electrons and gain stability because the shell below the valence shell is full of electrons. Elements in group 1 lose one electron and have a charge of +1. The elements in group 2 lose two electrons and form +2 charges, and the elements in group 13 form +3 charges. The charges for the transition metals vary.

The nonmetals are closer to the right side of the periodic table and have more than four valence electrons. Therefore, nonmetals tend to gain electrons in ionic bonds or share electrons in covalent bonds. Elements in group 14 bond covalently. Those in groups 15, 16, and 17 form -3, -2, and -1 charges, respectively. The elements in group 18 are known as the *noble gases*. They have a full valence shell and do not bond with other elements.

Connections

The elements in group 1 of the periodic table are known as the *alkali metals*. Alkali metals only have one valence electron and are not stable in their natural state. The reactivity of the alkali metals increases as you move down the group, making lithium the least reactive and francium the most reactive. These elements are so reactive that they will react explosively with water. When an alkali metal reacts with water, it causes the water molecules to split and release hydrogen gas into the air. The heat from the reaction often causes the hydrogen gas, also very reactive, to ignite. Because of the extreme reactivity of the alkali metals, they must be stored under special conditions. The less reactive metals like lithium, potassium, and sodium can be stored in a container of mineral oil. The more reactive metals require storage in pressurized tubes filled with noble gases.

Want to Know More?

See appendix for Our Findings.

Further Reading

Bentor, Yinon. Chemical Elements.com, 2009. Available online. URL: http://www.chemicalelements.com/index.html. Accessed July 17, 2010. This interactive periodic table provides information about all the elements, including the alkali metals in group 1.

Cyberspace Chemistry. "Lewis Dot Structures." Available online. URL: http://www.science.uwaterloo.ca/~cchieh/cact/c120/dotstruc.html. Accessed July 17, 2010. This Web site gives the history of Lewis dot structures and explains how to draw them.

McClinton, Martin, and Miriam Douglass. "Lewis Dot Structures of Covalent Compounds," 2010. Wisc-Online. Available online. URL: http://www.wisc-online.com/objects/ViewObject.aspx?ID=GCH6404. Accessed July 17, 2010. This PowerPoint presetation of covalent bonding provides helpful diagrams.

5. Making Soap

Topic

Basic soap can be made from oils and sodium hydroxide, then personalized with fragrant oils.

Introduction

Hundreds of varieties of soap can be found in your local pharmacy or grocery store. Products range from abrasive industrial soap to colorful and decorative soaps that are shaped in molds and liquid soap sold in pump bottles. Until the early 20th century, soap was almost entirely made at home using animal fats and a strong base called *lye* (sodium hydroxide) that was obtained from wood ash. The industrial production of soap began after World War I. At that time, fats were in short supply, so vegetable oils were used. Today, some people still choose to make their own soap so that they can select the properties of that soap.

The process of making soap is a type of neutralization reaction known as *saponification*. Neutralization is important because, without it, the acids and bases in soap would be dangerous to handle. In a *neutralization reaction*, an acid and a base react to form water and a neutral substance called a *salt*. Neutralization makes the acids and bases safe to use. Saponification requires a reaction between a slightly acidic oil and a very strong base to produce a salt with unique cleaning properties.

Soap can have different characteristics and qualities depending on the oils used to create it, as well as the scents, colors, and other additives that can be mixed in before the soap hardens. In this experiment, you will choose a combination of oils, colors, and fragrances and create soap using the process of saponification.

 **Time Required**

45 minutes

Materials

- 100 percent lye pellets (NaOH)
- olive oil (about 30 ounces [oz] [887 milliliters (ml)])
- canola oil (about 30 oz [887 ml])
- corn oil (about 30 oz [887 ml])
- palm oil (solid at room temperature) (about 30 oz [887 ml])
- coconut oil (solid at room temperature) (about 30 oz (887 ml)
- various scented oils (such as essential oils, citrus oils, and mint oils) in small bottles with droppers
- food coloring
- 11 oz (325 ml) distilled water
- small beaker
- large beaker
- hot plate
- thermometer
- large mixing bowl (glass or plastic, not metal)
- electronic balance
- stirring rod
- stick hand blender
- soap molds (plastic, cardboard, or wood; not metal)
- wax paper
- spatula
- knife
- measuring spoon (1 tablespoon [tbsp])
- measuring cup
- dropper bottle of phenolphthalein
- goggles

- hot mitts
- plastic pipettes
- 2 test tubes
- rubber gloves
- science notebook

Safety Note   Goggles must be worn at all times during this experiment. Wear rubber gloves and use caution when handling lye. Keep vinegar available for neutralization of lye spills. Use hot mitts when handling hot objects. Please review and follow the safety guidelines at the beginning of this volume.

Procedure

1. Place a small beaker onto an electronic balance. Set the units to ounces and tare the scale. Carefully measure out 4.65 oz (137.52 ml) of lye by adding it slowly into the beaker.

2. Use the measuring cup to measure 11 oz (325.31 ml) of distilled water. Pour the distilled water into a large beaker.

3. Carefully add the lye to the water. (Do not add water to lye, as it can cause a dangerous reaction). Stir gently until all of the lye crystals have dissolved. Use caution, as the beaker will be hot.

4. Remove a small sample of the lye mixture with a pipette and place it in a test tube. Add a drop of phenolphthalein indicator. Record any color change in your science notebook.

5. Place a thermometer into the lye mixture beaker, then set the beaker aside.

6. Decide on an oil mixture for your soap. You may mix and match oils, using as many types as you would like, but your total weight of all oils together (not including the scents) should be 30 oz (887.21 ml) (The oil that you use in the largest quantity should be a liquid at room temperature.)

7. Measure the 30 oz (887.21 ml) of oils you have selected. If some of your selections are solids, place them into a large beaker and heat slowly on a hot plate until melted, stirring frequently. Once the solid(s) have melted, slowly add them to the liquid oil(s). Place a thermometer into the mixture and bring the temperature up to 100

to 110 degrees Fahrenheit (°F) (38 to 43 degrees Celsius [°C]), then remove from the heat.

8. Once the oil mixture and lye mixture have both cooled to approximately 100°F (38°C), slowly add the lye mixture to the oil mixture while stirring.

9. Blend the mixture with a stick blender until it is evenly mixed and has thickened so that a drip of the mixture leaves a trace along the surface of the liquid that does not immediately disappear.

10. Add 1 to 2 tbsp of fragrance oil to the soap mixture and blend.

11. Add 1 to 4 drops of color to the mixture, if desired. Blend well for even color, or stir slowly for a swirled appearance.

12. Remove a small amount of the soap mixture on a spatula and place in a test tube. Add a drop of phenolphthalein, an acid-base indicator that remains clear in acidic conditions but turns bright pink if the pH rises above 8.2. If the indicator remains clear or turns a pale pink, the soap will be safe to use on your skin when the process is complete. If it turns bright pink, it will be too basic for use on the skin. It may be used on clothing or as a cleaning agent instead.

13. Line the soap mold with wax paper (unless using a waxed milk or juice carton).

14. Pour the soap mixture into a mold and allow to set for at least 24 hours.

15. The soap can be removed from the mold and sliced after 1 day, but should be allowed to cure for 2 weeks before using.

16. Observe the characteristics of your soap, such as texture and odor. After the soap has cured for a few weeks, test its lathering capabilities.

Analysis

1. What were the indications that a chemical reaction occurred in this experiment?

2. Describe the appearances of the lye solution and the oil solution before they were mixed. How did that change after they were combined?

3. How did the phenolphthalein react with the lye solution? With your soap solution?

4. What did the color of the phenolphthalein indicate about the pH of the solutions as the reaction progressed?

5. What do you think might happen if too much lye were used in this lab? If too little were used?

What's Going On?

Soap works because the molecule has a hydrocarbon "tail" that mixes with oil and other nonpolar substances and a polar "head" region that mixes with water (see Figure 1). The tail region is considered *hydrophobic* because it will not mix with water, while the head region is *hydrophilic*, or water-loving. Water is not an effective cleaner for oily materials because oil and water do not mix. The addition of soap to water enables the oily substances to dissolve in water and be washed away. Soap is described as an *emulsifier* because of its ability to break up oils and trap them inside *micelles*. These small spheres are formed from many soap molecules that turn their hydrophobic tails inward so that only the hydrophilic heads face the water (see Figure 2). The oil and dirt are thus surrounded and can be rinsed away with water.

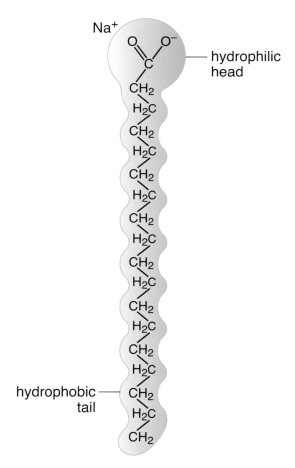

Figure 1

A soap molecule has a hydrophilic head and a hydrophobic tail.

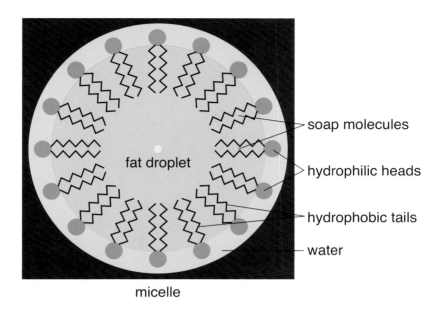

micelle

Figure 2

Soap interacts with fat or oil, forming a micelle.

Oils are made up of molecules called *triglycerides* which are composed of a *glycerol* unit, to which three *fatty acids* are attached. When triglycerides react with sodium hydroxide, the glycerol molecule is removed, leaving a negatively charged end on the fatty acid. This polar fatty acid attracts the positively charged sodium ions from the sodium hydroxide. The glycerol molecule is attracted to the oxygen and hydrogen from the sodium hydroxide (see Figure 3). When soaps are made commercially, the glycerol is usually extracted so that it can be used in creating other products. However, in homemade soap, the glycerol is retained, which tends to give the soap more skin-moisturizing properties.

Connections

Detergents are similar to soaps, but are produced synthetically. They were first developed during World War I because there was a shortage of the animal fats that were used to produce soap. Detergents are *surfactants* like soap, but they have a different structure. Detergents have hydrophilic and hydrophobic regions like soap, which enables them to attract dirt and oils, dissolve them in water, and allow them to be washed away. Where soaps are formed from triglycerides, detergents are often produced from *petrochemicals*, which are derived from petroleum, or *oleochemicals,* the products of plants or animals.

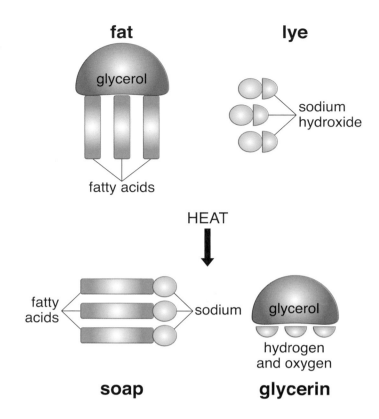

Figure 3

The saponification process

Detergents are not affected by the presence of minerals in the water, so unlike soaps, they work well in hard water and generally do not form soap scum. Modern detergents are manufactured to contain many additives such as enzymes to break down stains and bleach to whiten clothes.

 Want to Know More?

See appendix for Our Findings.

Further Reading

Miller, Kathy. "Miller's Homemade Soap Pages," 2007. Available online. URL: http://www.millersoap.com/. Accessed July 17, 2010. Miller is a veteran soap maker who provides troubleshooting suggestions for novices on her Web site.

Ophardt, Charles E. "Soap," 2003. Virtual ChemBook. Available online. URL: http://www.elmhurst.edu/~chm/vchembook/554soap.html. Accessed July 17, 2010. Opardt explains how soap molecules are created in hydrolysis reactions.

Parrish, Dennis. "Emulsion Polymerization," 2005. Available online. URL: http://pslc.ws/macrog/emulsion.htm. Accessed July 17, 2010. Parrish explains the chemistry of soap, including the formation of micelles in his "learning center."

"Soap and Detergents," April 2008. Available online. URL: http://www.newworldencyclopedia.org/entry/soap. Accessed July 17, 2010. This Web page outlines the history of soapmaking from ancient Babylon and Rome and explains the chemistry of soap.

6. Ozone Depletion

Topic

Student-designed models can be used to demonstrate the mechanism of ozone depletion.

Introduction

The Sun is the source of all energy for our planet. However, the *ultraviolet (UV) radiation* produced by the Sun is very powerful and can cause a great deal of damage. The *stratosphere* of the Earth's atmosphere contains a combination of gases that form a protective layer against the most harmful solar rays. One of the gases found in the stratosphere is *ozone*, a compound of three oxygen molecules (O_3), that prevents much of the ultraviolet radiation from reaching Earth's surface. Ozone is naturally created, broken down, and replenished within the atmosphere. First, molecules of O_2 react with UV radiation, causing them to split into very reactive single oxygen atoms. These atoms attach to O_2 molecules in the stratosphere, creating O_3 (see Figure 1).

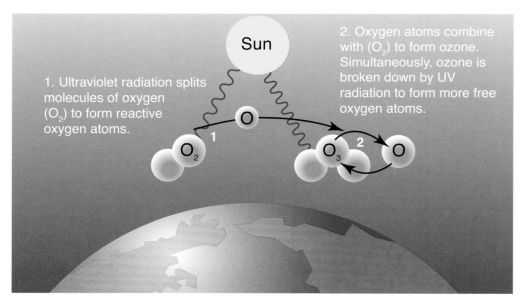

Figure 1

This protective ozone layer has undergone significant deterioration over the past 30 years as a result of man-made chemicals that have been released into the atmosphere. One of the most damaging groups of chemical is the *chlorofluorocarbons*, or CFCs. UV radiation causes chlorine atoms to break free from CFC molecules. The free chlorine atoms react with ozone, causing one oxygen atom to be removed from the molecule. The reacted oxygen breaks free from chlorine and joins to another free oxygen, forming O_2 instead of ozone (see Figure 2). The free chlorine atoms remain in the atmosphere and continue to react with ozone for an extended period of time. In this experiment, you will research the process of ozone depletion and build a three-dimensional model demonstrating the process of ozone depletion in the atmosphere.

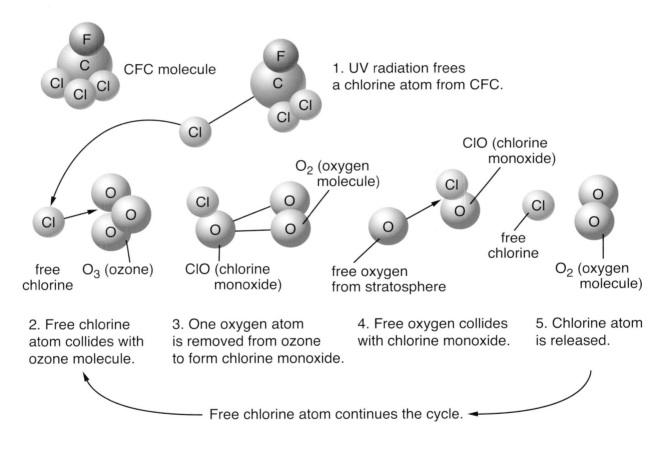

Figure 2

Time Required

45 minutes

Materials

- ⟜ access to the Internet
- ⟜ modeling clay (4 to 6 colors)
- ⟜ Styrofoam™ balls (various sizes)
- ⟜ tempera paint (4 to 6 colors)
- ⟜ toothpicks
- ⟜ pipe cleaners
- ⟜ poster board
- ⟜ colored markers
- ⟜ glue
- ⟜ science notebook

Safety Note Please review and follow the safety guidelines at the beginning of this volume.

Procedure

1. Access the Internet to learn more about the breakdown of ozone by CFCs. Record your findings in your science notebook. As you conduct your research, find the answers to Analysis questions 1 through 6.

2. Using the information you gathered, design a three-dimensional model that demonstrates the process of ozone depletion.

3. You can use any of the supplies provided by your teacher, but you will not need to use all of them.

4. Before you begin, decide exactly what you are going to do. Write the steps you plan to take (your procedure) and the materials you plan to use (materials list) on the data table. Show your procedure and materials list to the teacher. If you get teacher approval, proceed with your model. If not, modify your work and show it to your teacher again.

5. Once you have teacher approval, assemble the materials you need and begin your procedure.

6. Answer Analysis questions 7 and 8.

Data Table	
Your procedure	
Your materials list	
Teacher's approval	

Analysis

1. Draw the structural formulas for O_2 and O_3, including all of the unshared electrons.

2. What causes oxygen to be unstable as a single atom?

3. Free chlorine atoms from CFCs react with O_3 but not O_2. Why do you think this is?

4. After chlorine combines with an oxygen molecule, the oxygen is transferred to a free radical. Explain why chlorine does not remain attached to the oxygen atom.

5. Research ultraviolet radiation. What are the different types of UV rays? How are they different?

6. What are the harmful effects of ultraviolet radiation?

7. In your model, what did you use to represent oxygen atoms? chlorine atoms? chemical bonds?

8. If you were to repeat this experiment, how would you improve your model?

What's Going On?

Two oxygen atoms can form a double bond, sharing two electrons and creating the relatively stable molecule O_2. Although O_2 is described as stable, it can be broken down over time by large amounts of ultraviolet radiation, creating very reactive single oxygen atoms that are called *free radicals*. These reactive oxygen atoms attach to O_2 molecules in the atmosphere, forming ozone. In the atmosphere, ozone absorbs harmful UVB radiation and converts it to heat. In this way, the layer of ozone in the upper stratosphere protects the Earth from very harmful radiation. Although ozone is naturally replenished, the process is slow.

The ozone layer has been damaged by chlorine atoms released from CFCs, which are very reactive and capable of quickly changing ozone into O_2. One chlorine atom can combine with about 100,000 ozone molecules before it is broken down. Ongoing damage to the ozone layer is being monitored by scientists. Above Antarctica, a large hole in the ozone layer has been increasing in size (see Figure 3). Some scientists believe that the hole occurs above Antarctica because the atmosphere there creates the ideal environment for the reactions to occur. Ice crystals tend to catalyze the breakdown of CFCs into reactive chlorine atoms, and the reaction with ozone is more efficient at cooler temperatures.

Once the effects of CFCs were fully understood, they were largely banned by 1996, but they had been used by industrialized nations for much of the 20th century. Since chlorine and CFCs are not easily broken down, they can stay in the stratosphere for about 50 years. This means that it will take a very long time for the hole in the ozone layer to heal.

Connections

One common misconception is that the hole in the ozone layer is related to the phenomenon of global warming. Although the hole in the

September 1981

September 1987

September 1993

September 1999

Figure 3

The dark blue region is Antarctica. The "ozone hole" can be seen as a purple area around the continent.

ozone layer can potentially cause higher temperatures due to increased radiation, it is not generally accredited with the increased global temperatures. Global warming is caused by the *greenhouse effect*, the trapping of the Sun's heat by a layer of "greenhouse gases" such as carbon dioxide and water vapor in the atmosphere. Combustion of fossil fuels such as petroleum and gasoline produces greenhouse gases.

Global warming has caused the average temperature of the Earth to increase by a few degrees over the past 100 years. On a global scale, a few degrees can make a huge difference. The increase in temperature has the ability to change weather patterns and drastically impact the organisms on Earth. A few degrees can determine whether the ice caps in the polar regions will remain solid or melt. Melting ice caps could cause extreme worldwide flooding along with the loss of Arctic habitats. Additionally, some organisms such as the coral, which are very sensitive to temperature changes, can become extinct. Loss of coral reefs would set a chain reaction into motion because reefs are important nursery and hatchery regions for the majority of marine species, including popular commercial fish such as tuna, cod, and salmon.

Want to Know More?

See appendix for Our Findings.

Further Reading

Beyond Discovery. "The Ozone Depletion Problem." National Academy of Science, 2009. Available online. URL: http://www.beyonddiscovery.org/content/view.article.asp?a=73. Accessed July 17, 2010. This Web site explains the formation of ozone, the role of CFCs in its damage, and the work performed by scientists to understand the phenomenon.

National Geographic. "Ozone Depletion," 2010. Available online. URL: http://environment.nationalgeographic.com/environment/global-warming/ozone-depletion-overview.html. Accessed July 17, 2010. This article summarizes the problem of ozone loss over Antarctica.

National Science Foundation. "Ice Crystal Model Aids Analysis of Ozone Depletion," March 6, 2010. Available online. URL: http://www.nsf.gov/cise/kdi/ideas/ozone.html. Accessed July 17, 2010. This article explains the role of ice crystals in the breakdown of ozone.

"Ozone Destruction." The Ozone Hole. Available online. URL: http://www.theozonehole.com/ozonedestruction.htm. Accessed July 17, 2010. Excellent graphics on this Web page show how ozone is destroyed in the stratosphere.

Sparling, Brien. "Basic Chemistry of Ozone Depletion," May 1, 2003. NASA Advanced Supercomputing Division. Available online. URL:http://www.nas.nasa.gov/About/Education/Ozone/chemistry.html. Accessed July 17, 2010. Sparling explains how CFCs damage ozone and convert it into oxygen on this Web page.

7. Catalysis of Hydrogen Peroxide

Topic

Catalysts change the rate at which chemical reactions occur.

Introduction

Catalysts are substances that speed up chemical reactions by lowering the *activation energy*, the amount of energy that is required for the reaction to begin. (The process of speeding up the reaction is called catalysis.) Some reactions take place very slowly because a lot of energy is needed to get them started. The presence of a catalyst provides a pathway requiring less activation energy so that the reaction can proceed easily (see Figure 1). During a chemical reaction, a catalyst is not changed or used up. As a result, catalysts can be reused repeatedly.

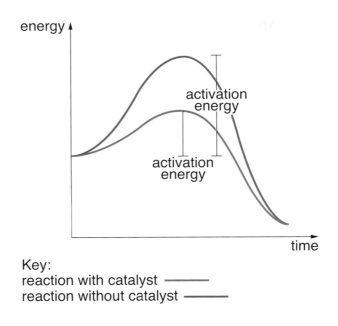

Figure 1

Catalysts speed up chemical reactions by reducing the amount of activation energy needed to get the reactions started.

Catalysts can take many forms. A *homogeneous* catalyst is in the same phase or state of matter as the reactants it is catalyzing. For example, a liquid catalyst in a reaction between liquids is a homogeneous catalyst. A *heterogeneous* catalyst is in a different phase than the reactants, such as a solid catalyst for a reaction between gases. In this experiment, you will observe the decomposition of hydrogen peroxide to water and oxygen both with and without a catalyst, manganese dioxide. The amount of hydrogen peroxide remaining will be tested by *titration* with potassium permanganate, a deep purple chemical that turns clear when reacted with hydrogen peroxide.

Time Required

30 minutes

Materials

- 6 percent hydrogen peroxide (H_2O_2) solution
- manganese dioxide (MnO_2) powder
- 2 percent potassium permanganate ($KMnO_4$) solution
- burette
- burette clamp
- ring stand
- funnel
- graduated cylinder
- 4 medium-size beakers
- spatula
- electronic balance
- plastic weigh boats
- stopwatch
- labeling tape
- goggles
- science notebook

Safety Note   Goggles must be worn at all times during this experiment. Manganese dioxide and potassium permanganate are strong oxidizing agents and may cause permanent staining of skin and clothing. Please review and follow the safety guidelines at the beginning of this volume.

Procedure

1. Label two beakers "with catalyst" and "without catalyst."

2. Measure 50 milliliters (ml) of 6 percent hydrogen peroxide and pour into a beaker. Repeat for the second beaker.

3. Place a plastic weigh boat on a balance and tare. Mass out 0.5 grams (g) of manganese dioxide into the weigh boat.

4. Add the manganese dioxide to the "with catalyst" beaker. Allow the substances to react until the bubbling slows.

5. Set up a burette on a ring stand with a burette clamp. Using a funnel, fill the burette with potassium permanganate. Use caution, as potassium permanganate will stain skin and clothing.

6. Remove 5 ml of the peroxide from the "without catalyst" beaker and add to a separate beaker.

7. Record the initial volume of the burette.

8. Titrate the hydrogen peroxide in the "without catalyst" beaker. To do so, add potassium permanganate to the beaker containing 5 ml of hydrogen peroxide, one drop at a time, until the solution in the beaker turns a very faint pink to brown color that lingers. Record the final volume of the burette on your data table. Keep these points in mind:

   ✔ If the solution turns dark pink, brown, or purple, you must start over with another 5 ml sample from the same beaker.

   ✔ It is not necessary to refill the burette between trials, but you must record the new initial volume before beginning.

   ✔ If the burette runs out of potassium permanganate, it will need to be refilled. Make sure that you keep track of the volume used before you refill the burette.

9. Subtract the initial volume from the final volume to determine the total volume of potassium permanganate used. Record the volume in the appropriate column of the data table.

10. Repeat the titration (steps 6 through 9) of the same solution until you have two very pale titrations. With each titration, record the volumes used on the data table.

11. Divide the total volume of potassium permanganate in both trials by 2 to find the average volume. Record the average volume in the last column of the data table.

12. Repeat steps 6 through 11 with 5 ml of solution from the "with catalyst" beaker.

Data Table					
		Initial volume of burette	Final volume of burette	Total volume of $KMnO_4$ used	Average volume of $KMnO_4$
With catalyst	Trial 1				
	Trial 2				
Without catalyst	Trial 1				
	Trial 2				

Analysis

1. Hydrogen peroxide (H_2O_2) breaks down into water and oxygen gas. Write the equation for this reaction.

2. Is manganese dioxide a homogeneous or heterogeneous catalyst? Explain your answer.

3. Describe the differences you could see between the catalyzed and uncatalyzed decomposition of hydrogen peroxide.

4. What is the purpose of the potassium permanganate in this reaction?

5. Calculate the average amount of $KMnO_4$ used to titrate each solution. Record these values on the data table.

6. How did the amount of potassium permanganate used to titrate the uncatalyzed hydrogen peroxide compare to the amount used to titrate the catalyzed reaction?

7. What does the amount of potassium permanganate indicate about the progress of the decomposition reaction?

What's Going On?

Hydrogen peroxide (H_2O_2) will naturally decompose into water (H_2O) and oxygen gas (O_2). However, this reaction is very slow unless a catalyst is added. Manganese (IV) oxide (MnO_2), commonly known as manganese dioxide, is a catalyst for the decomposition of hydrogen peroxide. The addition of manganese dioxide to hydrogen peroxide shows visible evidence of a chemical reaction because the oxygen gas forms bubbles as it is released from the solution.

Potassium permanganate ($KMnO_4$) reacts with hydrogen peroxide in an *oxidation-reduction (redox) reaction*. Hydrogen peroxide *oxidizes* potassium permanganate, which changes the color of the solution from deep purple to clear. When the hydrogen peroxide molecules have all reacted, the potassium permanganate will begin to turn the solution back to its original deep purple color. In this reaction, the addition of potassium permanganate was stopped at the point where the solution began to turn slightly pink or brown, indicating that all of the hydrogen peroxide had reacted. Therefore, the amount of hydrogen peroxide that remained in the solution and had not been decomposed by the reaction could be determined.

Connections

Biological catalysts that speed up the reactions in living things are known as *enzymes.* These molecules are proteins that catalyze chemical reactions within the body. Enzymes are specific to one particular type of reaction and are often named after the reaction they catalyze. For instance, the enzyme *lactase* helps to break down the sugar lactose, which is found in milk. The substance with which an enzyme reacts, such as lactose, is known as a *substrate*. Enzymes and their substrates fit together perfectly, very much like a lock and key (see Figure 2). The area of an enzyme that fits with substrates is known as the *active site*. As substrates fit into the active site, the enzyme enables the substrates to undergo a specific chemical reaction.

Enzymes, like all proteins, can only function properly within a specific range of conditions. Changes in pH or temperature can cause enzymes to *denature*. Once an enzyme is denatured, it changes shape and the active site is deformed. If the shape of an active site can no longer fit with the substrate, then the enzyme is unable to catalyze the reaction.

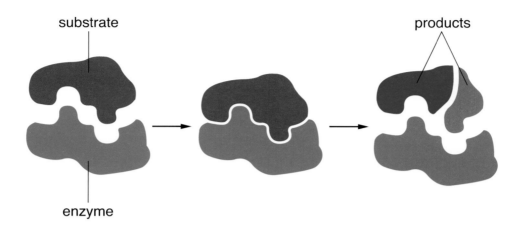

Figure 2

An enzyme and its substrate fit together the way a key fits a lock. Once in position on the enzyme, a substrate can undergo a chemical reaction.

Want to Know More?

See appendix for Our Findings.

Further Reading

Clark, Jim. "The Effects of Catalysts on Reaction Rates," 2002. ChemGuide. Available online. URL: http://www.chemguide.co.uk/ physical/basicrates/catalyst.html. Accessed July 17, 2010. Clark explains how catalysts work and gives several examples on this Web page.

Rader, Andrew. "Catalysts Speed It Up," 2009. Chem4Kids.com. Available online. URL: http://www.chem4kids.com/files/react_catalyst.html. Accessed July 17, 2010. On this Web page, Rader explains the activity of enzymes in simple language and provides helpful figures to illustrate his explanation.

Royal Society of Chemistry. "Enzymes," *Chemistry for Biologists,* 2004. Available online. URL: http://www.rsc.org/education/teachers/learnnet/ cfb/enzymes.htm. Accessed July 17, 2010. This chapter in a Web textbook discusses the structure of enzymes, their active sites, and factors that denature enzymes.

Using Hydrogen Peroxide. "Elephant Toothpaste—a hydrogen peroxide chemistry experiment," 2008. Available online. URL: http://www.using-hydrogen-peroxide.com/elephant-toothpaste.html. Accessed July 17, 2010. Videos on this Web site compare the decomposition of hydrogen peroxide with and without a catalyst.

Yasuda, Catherine. "Introduction to Catalysts," November 29, 2008. YouTube. Available online. URL: http://www.youtube.com/watch?=5nCK uafgbT8&feature=related. Accessed July 17, 2010. In this video tutorial, Yasuda explains how a catalyst speeds up a chemical reaction.

8. Wood Alcohol

Topic

Wood can undergo decomposition to produce methyl alcohol.

Introduction

Throughout much of history, wood has been used as a fuel. Burning wood can give rise to many different compounds, including charcoal, methyl alcohol, and a mixture of particles that can build up to create *creosote*, or tar residue. Methyl alcohol, also called methanol or wood alcohol, is a very simple but useful alcohol with the formula CH_3OH (see Figure 1).

Methanol can be used as a fuel for automobiles, a *solvent*, and a type of antifreeze. This alcohol can be isolated from burning wood through the process of *destructive distillation* in which wood is strongly heated so that it decomposes. Tar, methanol, and acetic acid condense in the distillation apparatus (see Figure 2) and the *volatile* gases are given off. In this experiment, you will decompose wood chips using destructive distillation in order to isolate methyl alcohol.

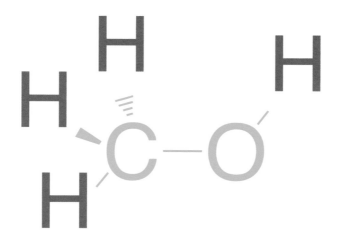

Figure 1

Structural formula for methanol (wood alcohol)

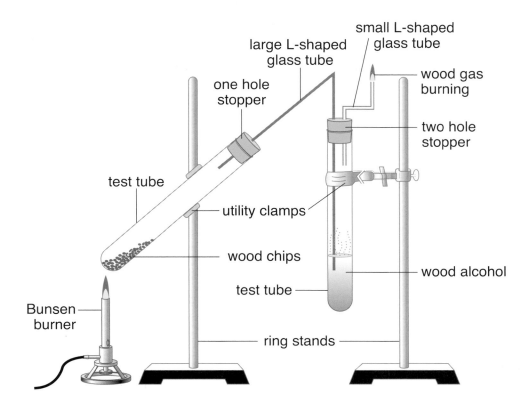

Figure 2

Time Required

45 minutes

Materials

- ◆ wood chips or shavings
- ◆ Bunsen burner
- ◆ flint striker
- ◆ 2 ring stands
- ◆ 2 utility clamps
- ◆ 2 large test tubes
- ◆ rubber stopper with 2 holes (to fit test tube)
- ◆ rubber stopper with 1 hole (to fit test tube)
- ◆ large L-shaped glass tubing

- small L-shaped glass tubing
- matches
- hot mitts
- goggles
- watch glass
- science notebook

Safety Note Goggles must be worn at all times during this experiment. Use extreme caution when working with fire and the flammable products formed in this lab. Use hot mitts when handling hot objects. Please review and follow the safety guidelines at the beginning of this volume.

Procedure

1. Set up the distillation apparatus as shown in Figure 2. As you do, keep these points in mind:
   a. The two test tubes should be connected to two ring stands with utility clamps.
   b. The test tube that will be heated should be placed horizontally or at an angle as shown in Figure 2. It will contain the stopper with a single hole. This test tube will be positioned over a Bunsen burner.
   c. The test tube that will collect the products will be placed vertically and have the stopper with two holes.
   d. The long piece of L-shaped glass tubing will connect the two test tubes.
   e. The short piece of L-shaped tubing will be placed into the second hole of the vertical test tube.
2. Fill the horizontal tube about one-fourth full with wood chips.
3. Light the Bunsen burner with a flint striker and place it directly below the wood chips in the test tube.
4. Heat the wood chips thoroughly so that they become completely charred.
5. Light a match in the mouth of the small L-shaped tube. Record your observations in your science notebook.

6. Once the wood has completely decomposed, turn off the Bunsen burner and observe the mixture in the condensation tube. Record your observations in your science notebook.

7. Allow the mixture in the condensation tube to cool, then carefully pour a small amount of the top layer of liquid onto a watch glass. Be very careful not to touch the liquid or directly inhale its vapor.

8. Place the watch glass on a heat proof surface. In order to test for the presence of methanol, light a match and carefully touch it to the liquid in the watch glass; the liquid should ignite. The flame will extinguish itself once the alcohol has been burned off.

Analysis

1. Describe the difference in appearance of the wood before and after burning it.

2. Observe the surfaces of the glass tubing in your apparatus. How did the appearance of the tubing change from the way it looked before the experiment? What caused this change?

3. What happened when you lit a match in the mouth of the open glass tubing? Why do you think this occurred?

4. Was methanol the only liquid formed in this lab? If not, describe the appearance of the other liquid(s).

5. Sketch a picture of the condensation tube that collected the liquid substances. Label the layers that formed with the substance that was contained in them.

6. Describe what happened when you ignited the liquid in the watch glass. Was the flame different from a Bunsen burner flame? From the flames formed when wood burns?

What's Going On?

When wood is burned completely, it forms charcoal, a black and brittle material. Charcoal is composed primarily of carbon, which is flammable and can be used as a source of heat and energy. Charcoal is very absorbent, so it is also used to purify air and water. In addition to charcoal, burned wood produces a variety of gases, primarily carbon monoxide and hydrogen gas, as well as many small particulates that form soot buildup on the glass surfaces. The gaseous components of burned wood are flammable and ignite easily. The particulate matter forms a yellow to brown buildup of flammable thick liquid known as *woodtar*.

The liquid products of the destructive distillation of wood include sticky, dark-colored tar, which is the most dense liquid produced, generally forming at the bottom of the condensation tube. In addition to the tar, decomposed wood yields a mixture of acetic acid and methanol known as *pyroligneeous acid*. This product can be used medicinally as a detoxifying agent as well as a pain reliever and sterilizing agent. Finally, wood's distillation yields methanol (wood alcohol), a solvent that is found in many everyday solutions such as windshield washing fluid. Methanol is extremely flammable and is toxic if ingested or inhaled.

Connections

Many homes have fireplaces that burn wood in order to provide warmth. However, such fireplaces can become very dangerous if not properly maintained. As wood burns, it produces flammable gases that contain particulate matter. The gases are transported outside of the home by a chimney. However, the gas cools as it rises toward open air and some of the particulate matter sticks to the interior of the chimney. The deposit is flammable and when large amounts accumulate, it can cause a very dangerous and destructive chimney fire. Once the deposit begins to burn, it often ignites explosively, causing extensive damage. For this reason, homeowners must keep chimneys clean, either by sweeping them out or burning specialized logs that break down the harmful buildup from the inner surfaces of a chimney.

Want to Know More?

See appendix for Our Findings.

Further Reading

Chemistry Daily. "Methanol," 2007. Available online. URL: http://www. chemistrydaily.com/chemistry/Methanol. Accessed July 17, 2010. This Web site reviews the chemistry of methanol production along with the history of this chemical.

"Methanol." Methanol Market Services Asia, 2010. Available online. URL: http://www.methanolmsa.com/exec/sam/view/id=183/node=115/. Accessed July 17, 2010. This Web site describes many of the uses of methanol, including its derivatives acetic acid and formaldehyde.

"Methanol." Paladin Labs, 2008. Available online. URL: http://www. antizol.com/mpoisono.htm. Accessed July 17, 2010. Methanol is a poison that can cause blindness and death. This article, available from the manufacturer of the antidote, reviews the toxic effects of this chemical.

"Methanol (compilation)," October 21, 2007. YouTube. Available online. URL: http://www.youtube.com/watch?=kdDEDr3HX7Y. Accessed July 17, 2010. A science teacher demonstrated methanol's flammability in this video.

"Methanol Vapor Burning in a Plastic Jug," 2009. Chemistry at Illinois. Available online. URL: http://www.chem.uiuc.edu/clcwebsite/meth. html. Accessed July 26, 2010. This Web site provides demonstration photographs of the combustion of methanol.

"Wood gas vehicles: firewood in the fuel tank," January 18, 2010. *Low-tech Magazine*. Available online. URL: http://www.lowtechmagazine. com/2010/01/wood-gas-cars.html. Accessed July 26, 2010. This article discusses the process of wood gasification to fuel cars, a common practice during World War II.

9. Solutes Affect the Boiling Point of Water

Topic

The boiling temperature of water varies depending on the solutes it contains.

Introduction

Have you ever added salt to boiling water when you are cooking? If so, you probably noticed that the salt increased the rate of boiling. To understand why this happens, you must first know a little about the characteristics of water. Water is a molecule that commonly exists as a solid, liquid, and a gas (see Figure 1). In the solid form, the molecules of water are locked into a low-energy crystalline shape. In the liquid state, the molecules are less constrained, so are able to flow past each other. Water molecules in the liquid phase undergo fairly strong interactions due to the *hydrogen bonds* that form between the slightly positive hydrogen atoms and the slightly negative oxygen atoms of adjacent atoms (see Figure 2). When molecules of water exist as a vapor, they contain a lot of energy and there are few interactions between molecules.

ice   liquid   water vapor

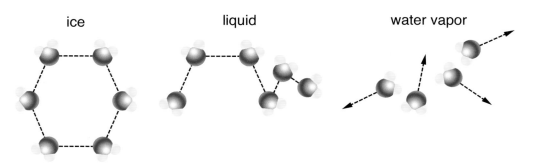

Figure 1

The arrangement of water molecules in the solid, liquid, and gaseous phases

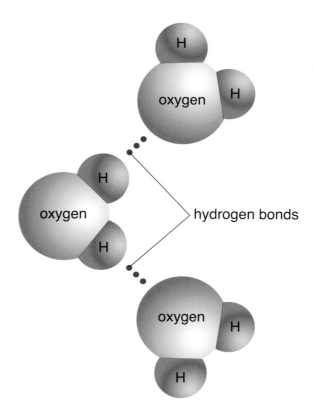

Figure 2

**In water, the slightly negatively charged oxygen molecules
are attracted to the slightly positively charged hydrogen molecules,
creating hydrogen bonds.**

The state of water depends on both pressure and temperature. At sea level, pure liquid water freezes to form solid ice at 32 degrees Fahrenheit (°F) (0 degrees Celsius [°C]) and boils to form vapor at 212°F (100°C). However, the addition of particles to water can affect its boiling and freezing points. Particles interfere with the ability of the water molecules to vaporize or freeze. In this laboratory, you will design an experiment to find the effects of three different chemicals on the temperature of boiling water.

Time Required

45 minutes

Materials

- hot plate
- distilled or deionized water (about 1 liter [L])
- 3 beakers (medium size)
- sodium chloride (NaCl) (about 50 grams [g])
- sugar ($C_{12}H_{22}O_{11}$) (about 50 g)
- calcium chloride ($CaCl_2$) (about 50 g)
- potassium chloride (KCl) (about 50 g)
- magnesium chloride ($MgCl_2$) (about 50 g)
- electronic balance
- measuring tablespoon
- 3 thermometers
- graduated cylinder
- goggles
- hot mitts
- science notebook

Safety Note   Goggles must be worn at all times during this experiment. Use caution when heating glassware and when using water and electrical appliances such as hot plates. Use hot mitts when handling hot objects. Please review and follow the safety guidelines at the beginning of this volume.

Procedure

1. Your job is to design and perform an experiment to compare the effects of three different solutes on the boiling point of water. The solutes available are sodium chloride, sugar, calcium chloride, potassium chloride, and magnesium chloride.

2. You can use any of the supplies provided by your teacher, but you will not need to use all of them.

3. Before you conduct your experiment, decide exactly what you are going to do. Write the steps you plan to take (your experimental procedure) and the materials you plan to use (materials list) on the data table below. Keep in mind that you need to control for *variables*. For example, you should use the same amount of water for each solute you test. In addition, you should boil some pure water as a comparison to the water containing solutes.

4. Show your procedure and materials list to the teacher. If you get teacher approval, proceed with your experiment. If not, modify your work and show it to your teacher again.

5. Once you have teacher approval, assemble the materials you need and begin your procedure.

6. Collect your results on a data table of your own design.

Data Table	
Your procedure	
Your materials list	
Teacher's approval	

Analysis

1. Which three solutes did you choose to test in this experiment? Why did you select them?

2. Describe the factors that you controlled. Why is it important to have controls in a science experiment?

3. How did the boiling temperatures of the water samples containing solutes compare to the boiling temperature of pure water?

4. Explain why you think you got the results that you did.

5. When dissolved in water, *ionic compounds* break up into individual *ions*. List the compounds that were used in your experiment and the number of particles each will break into.

6. Create a graph plotting the boiling temperature of each solution versus the number of particles formed in a solution. Connect the dots with a line. What trend do you see?

7. How is the boiling temperature related to the number of particles in a solute?

What's Going On?

The boiling point of water changes when solutes are added. The magnitude of this change depends on the number of particles that are present after the solute dissolves. *Covalent compounds* such as sugar do not dissociate into ions; ionic compounds such as sodium chloride (table salt) do. The boiling point elevation of water is known as a *colligative property*, one that depends on the number of molcules in solution rather than the properties of those molecules. Examples of colligative properties include boiling point, freezing point, and vapor point. The properties of *vapor point* depression and boiling point elevation are very closely related to each other. The vapor pressure is determined by the number of solvent molecules existing as a gas directly above a solution (see Figure 3). In order to evaporate, the solvent particles must be in contact with the surface of the solution. The presence of solute particles in a solution decreases the number of solvent molecules that can be at the surface of the solution, which lowers the vapor pressure and raises the boiling point. Therefore, water in the solution must be heated to a higher temperature in order for evaporation to occur.

The change in the boiling point of a solution containing solutes depends on the number of particles that exist in a solution. Since ionic compounds

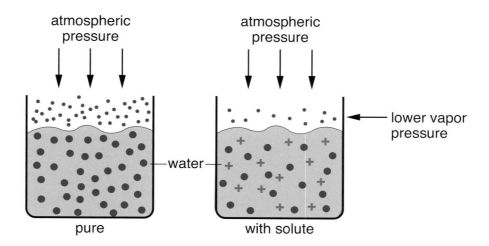

Figure 3

The addition of solutes to water reduces vapor pressure and raises boiling point.

break up into individual ions, they affect colligative properties more than covalent compounds. Likewise, compounds that form more than two particles when they dissociate affect the colligative properties more than those that simply break into two particles.

Connections

Freezing point depression is a type of colligative property like boiling point elevation and vapor pressure reduction. When water freezes, it forms a crystalline structure. The addition of solutes to water prevents the water molecules from forming an organized pattern. Because of this, the temperature must be much lower than normal for the water to freeze. An example of this colligative property can be seen during the winter when temperatures drop below freezing. Salt can be applied to sidewalks and roadways to help melt the ice. The salt separates the water molecules and causes the freezing point to be much lower than 32°F (0°C). Reducing the ice on surfaces helps prevent injuries and automobile accidents.

Want to Know More?

See appendix for Our Findings.

Further Reading

"Chemistry Explained," 2010. Adameg Incorporated. Available online. URL: http://www.chemistryexplained.com/Ce-Co/Colligative-Properties. html. Accessed July 17, 2010. This Web site explains how solutes affect freezing point and includes a formula for calculating freezing point depression.

Chemtutor. "Solutions," 2009. Available online. URL: http://www. chemtutor.com/solution.htm. Accessed July 17, 2010. This Web site reviews colligative properties and other topics related to solutions.

Hyperphysics. "Boiling Point Elevation in Solution." Available online. URL: http://hyperphysics.phy-astr.gsu.edu/hbase/Chemical/boilpt.html. Accessed July 17, 2010. Hyperphysics is a Web site that was developed by Georgia State University to help students of the physical sciences understand complex subjects. This page discusses how the addition of solutes increases boiling point.

10. Potable Water

Topic

Commercial techniques can be used in the laboratory to purify water.

Introduction

Clear, sparkling water flowing in a stream may appear to be pure, but it most likely contains contaminants. According to the Environmental Protection Agency, about 90 percent of the world's water is contaminated in some way. Water can be contaminated by many different sources, including nitrates from fertilizers and animal wastes, chemicals such as *polychlorinated biphenyls (PCB)* and *benzene* from industrial processes, gasoline from leaky tanks, chlorine and fluorine from water treatment plants, copper and lead from pipes, and organic wastes from septic tanks (see Figure 1). In addition, disease-causing microorganisms such as bacteria and *protozoans* inhabit many waterways. Therefore, as a precaution, water should be purified before it is consumed.

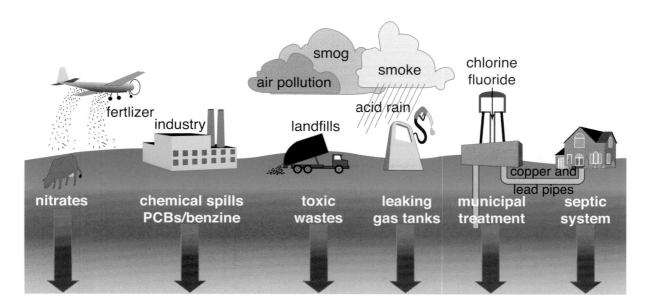

Figure 1

Potential sources of water contamination

Municipal water purification plants employ a variety of technique to make water *potable*, or safe to drink. Water is first filtered through a series of screens in order to filter out debris, then it is treated with chemicals to remove or neutralize harmful substances such as heavy metals and fertilizers. Solid substances are allowed to *precipitate* out of the water, and then water is filtered and disinfected before it is sent to reservoirs to be stored for use in homes. Figure 2 shows the steps of purification in a generalized water plant. Water is taken in from a stream or other source, then filtered to remove debris and grit. Once in the purification plant, water is treated with chemicals, mixed, and sent to the flocculator, a tank in which the chemicals and impurities interact to form soft, lumpy precipitates. The precipitates are allowed to settle out, then removed by sand filtration. After the filtered water is disinfected, it is sent to reservoirs until needed.

When a municipal purification system is not available, similar processes can be used on a much smaller scale. In this experiment you will perform four different methods of water purification: boiling, filtration, adding bleach, and adding iodine. Then, using a water test kit, you will compare the effectiveness of the four methods.

Time Required

60 minutes

Materials

- water from an outdoor source (groundwater or water from a lake, river, or stream) (about 1.6 quarts [qt]) (1.5 liters [L]))
- bleach (sodium hypochlorite) (few drops)
- iodine (2 percent tincture solution) (few drops)
- hot plate
- funnel
- filter paper (or cone coffee filters)
- activated carbon (charcoal) (about 1/2 cup [c])
- 4 beakers (250 milliliter [ml] or larger)
- graduated cylinder
- hot mitts

- ⚬ droppers
- ⚬ stirring rods
- ⚬ drinking water test kit (recommended: First Alert™ test kit)
- ⚬ science notebook

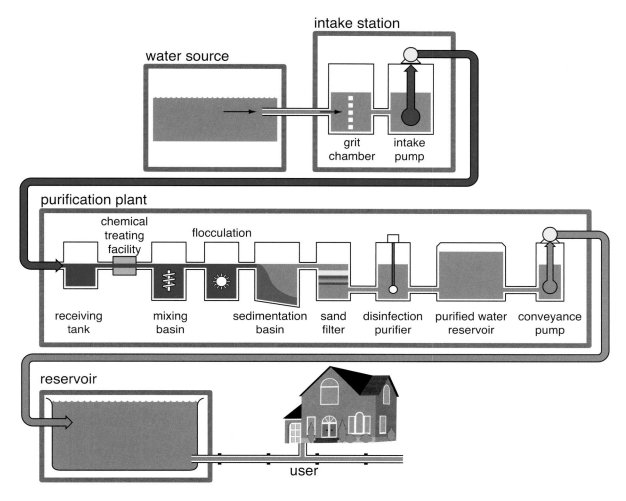

Figure 2

Municipal water filtration process

Procedure

1. Obtain about 1.6 qt (1.5 L) of water from an outdoor source.

2. Use the drinking water test kit to test a sample of the water for the presence of bacteria, lead, fertilizers, nitrates/nitrites, pH, hardness, and chlorine. Record the results obtained from each test on the data table.

3. Answer Analysis questions 1 and 2.

4. Label four clean beakers with the purification method that will be used on the water in them: boiling, filtration, bleach, and iodine.

5. Pour 250 ml of water into each of the labeled beakers. Purify the water in each beaker using the following directions:

Boiling:

   a. Place the beaker of water on a hot plate.
   b. Turn on the hot plate and heat the water to boiling.
   c. Allow water to boil for 10 minutes.
   d. Turn the hot plate off and allow the water to cool.

Filtration:

   a. Place a piece of filter paper or a coffee filter into a funnel.
   b. Fill the funnel about one-half full with activated carbon.
   c. Place the funnel in the mouth of a clean, empty beaker.
   d. Slowly pour the water sample into the funnel so that it passes through the carbon and the paper filter.
   e. Collect the filtered water from the bottom beaker.

Bleach:

   a. Add 5 drops of bleach to the beaker.
   b. Stir with a stirring rod for at least 30 seconds.
   c. Allow the water to sit for 10 minutes before testing.

Iodine:

   a. Add 5 drops of iodine tincture to the beaker.
   b. Stir with a stirring rod for at least 30 seconds.
   c. Allow the water to sit for 10 minutes before testing.

6. Test the water in each of the four beakers as you did with the original water sample in step 2. Record your results on the data table.

Data Table					
	Untreated	**Boiling**	**Filtration**	**Bleach**	**Iodine**
Bacteria					
Lead					
Fertilizers					
Nitrates/ nitrites					
pH					
Hardness					
Chlorine					

Analysis

1. Which contaminants were found in the sample of untreated water that you used in this experiment?

2. Which treatment do you predict will be the most effective in removing impurities? Why?

3. Could you notice visible changes in the water purity when you treated it with any of the four methods? If so, which one(s)?

4. Which treatment removed the most contaminants?

5. Which method(s) would be the most effective in removing microorganisms from water?

6. Which method(s) would be the most effective in removing chemical agents from water?

7. Water quality includes not only the purity of water but also the taste. Which treatment or combination of treatments do you think would produce the safest and best tasting water?

What's Going On?

The effectiveness of different forms of water purification largely depends on the type of contaminants found in the water. Boiling kills microorganisms and may help to precipitate some solid contaminants. Distillation, or boiling and condensing the water vapor, is more effective at purifying water, but it is not very convenient because it takes more time and requires specialized equipment. Filtration can remove sediment and make water more clear. If the filter contains activated carbon, it can help to remove ions and metal contaminants as well. Chlorine bleach and iodine can be used to kill microorganisms in water and help to neutralize and precipitate chemicals, but the treated water must sit for a period of time before it can be consumed. Techniques such as adding bleach and iodine are more effective when combined with filtration to remove any particles that settle out. Additionally, some people find the taste of treated water undesirable.

Connections

Some of the most dangerous contaminants of water are parasitic protozoans, one-celled organisms that are capable of movement during some stage of their life cycle. Because these organisms are unicellular, they cannot be seen with the naked eye, so it is impossible to tell if a sample of water is contaminated simply by looking at it. In fact, many protozoans exist in clear streams and fast-moving water that some individuals might assume to be safe. Most protozoans are so small that they cannot be removed by simple filtration, but they can be removed by chemical treatment or boiling.

Some parasitic protozoa found in water are *Giardia*, *Entamoeba,* and *Cryptosporidium*. *Giardia* (see Figure 3) is the most common cause of extreme vomiting and diarrhea among hikers and campers in the wilderness. *Entamoeba* can cause amoebic dysentery, also known as "Montezuma's revenge" or "travelers diarrhea." This organism is more common in nonindustrialized countries and most often affects tourists and travelers to those areas who consume the water. *Cryptosporidium* is not as well-known as the other protozoans, but has been known to contaminate municipal water sources in industrialized areas, causing diarrhea and intestinal problems for consumers.

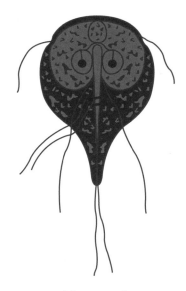

Figure 3

Giardia is a protozoan found in water that causes vomiting and diarrhea.

Want to Know More?

See appendix for Our Findings.

Further Reading

Centers for Disease Control. "Giardiasis (*Giardia* Infection)," October 5, 2009. Available online. URL: http://www.cdc.gov/ncidod/dpd/parasites/ Giardiasis/factsht_giardia.htm. Accessed July 17, 2010. This Web page provides information on how giardiasis is transmitted, its symptoms, and treatment.

Environmental Protection Agency. "Emergency Disinfection of Drinking Water," November 28, 2006. Available online. URL: http://www.epa. gov/safewater/faq/emerg.html. Accessed July 17, 2010. This Web site explains how to disinfect water in emergency situations.

Utah Division of Water Resources. "Drinking Water." Available online. URL: http://www.watereducation.utah.gov/WaterInUtah/Municipal/default. asp. Accessed July 17, 2010. This Web site explains how water sources are identified and how water from those sources is treated for human consumption.

11. Solutions and Spectrophotometry

Topic

A spectrophotometer can be used to analyze the transmission of light through different solutions.

Introduction

Solutions are types of *homogenous* mixtures in which one substance, the *solute*, is dissolved in a *solvent*. Solutions can be described as concentrated, where there is a large amount of solute dissolved in a solvent, or dilute, where there is a small amount of solute. However, these descriptions are qualitative and are generally not very precise. Solutions can also be described quantitatively by using *molarity* (M), the number of *moles* (mol) of solute per liter of solution. A solution with a high molarity is more concentrated than one with a low molarity.

Many chemical solutions are transparent, and the molarity cannot be known simply by looking at the solutions' color. However, with some solutions, the color of the solution changes as the concentration changes. In these cases, the solutions can be analyzed using a *spectrophotometer* (Figure 1a). Inside a spectrophotometer, a beam of light passes through a *monochromator*, a device that changes the beam so that it is made up of only one wavelength of light. This modified beam travels through the sample to be tested, which is held in a *cuvette*, a thin glass tube. A sensor on the other side of the sample detects the light, and the device calculates the amount of light that is transmitted and the amount absorbed by the solution (Figure 1b). In this experiment, you will create copper (II) sulfate solutions of known concentrations, then test their absorbance using a spectrophotometer. You will use your data to create a graph of concentration versus light absorbance. Then, using the graph you created, you will determine the concentration of an unknown solution of copper (II) sulfate.

Time Required

60 minutes

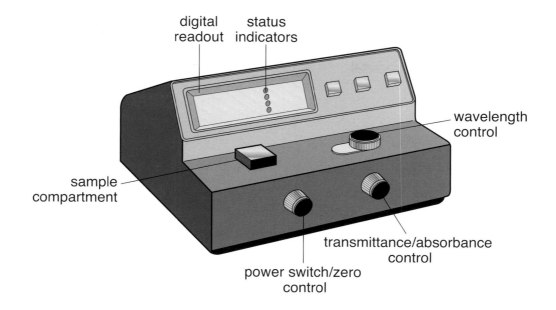

a. spectrophotometer

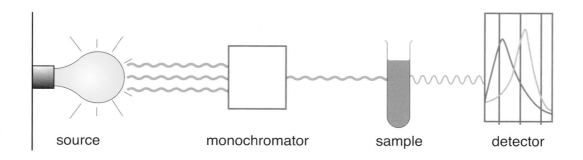

b. the spectrophotometry process

Figure 1

Materials

- spectrophotometer
- cuvettes
- small beakers
- distilled water
- lens wipes

- 1 molar (M) copper (II) sulfate ($CuSO_4$) solution
- copper (II) sulfate solution of unknown concentration (between 0.1 and 1.0 M)
- 10-milliliter (ml) volumetric flask with stopper
- graduated cylinder
- test-tube rack
- graph paper
- goggles
- science notebook

Safety Note Goggles must be worn at all times during this experiment. Use caution when using chemicals. Please review and follow the safety guidelines at the beginning of this volume.

Procedure

1. Turn on the spectrophotometer and allow it to warm up.

2. Label six cuvettes on the top rim with the following: 0 M, 0.25 M, 0.5 M, 0.75 M, 1.0 M, and unknown. Place the cuvettes in a test-tube rack.

3. Your teacher will provide a 1.0 M solution of copper (II) sulfate and distilled water (0.0 M). You will need to prepare the 0.25 M, 0.5 M, and 0.75 M solutions of copper (II) sulfate by performing dilutions of the 1.0 M solution. To do so:

    a. Use the formula $M_1V_1=M_2V_2$, where V equals volume, to calculate the volume of 1.0 M solution you will need to produce 10-ml solutions with the desired concentrations (0.25 M, 0.5 M, and 0.75 M). Record your calculated values in the last column of Data Table 1.

    b. Measure out the calculated volume of 1.0 M $CuSO_4$ needed for the 0.25 M dilution using a graduated cylinder.

    c. Carefully pour the measured amount of solution into a 10 ml volumetric flask and dilute up to the line with distilled water. Place the stopper in the flask and invert several times to mix.

    d. Pour the solution into a small labeled beaker and set aside for use in step 4.

    e. Repeat the dilution (steps b through d) for the two remaining (0.5 M and 0.75 M) dilutions.

4. Using a graduated cylinder, measure 2 ml of distilled water and add it to the 0.0 M cuvette. Repeat with 2 ml of each of the remaining known solutions (0.25 M, 0.5 M, 0.75 M, and 1.0 M) and the unknown solution obtained from your teacher.

5. Answer Analysis questions 1 and 2.

6. Set the wavelength on the spectrophotometer to 610 nanometers (nm) (refer to Figure 1a) and switch the mode to measure absorbance, not transmittance. Be sure that the sample cover is empty and closed, then turn the zeroing knob to "0 percent."

7. Clean the outer surface of the 0.0 M distilled water cuvette with a lens wipe to ensure that there are no fingerprints on the part of the tube that will be read.

8. Place the 0.0 M cuvette into the sample well of the spectrophotometer and close the lid. This tube will serve as your "blank." Set the control knob to "0 percent absorbance." Remove the cuvette and return it to the test-tube rack.

9. Wipe the 0.25 M cuvette and place it in the sample well. Close the lid and wait for the absorbance reading to stabilize. Record the percentage absorbance reading on Data Table 2. Remove the cuvette and return it to the test-tube rack.

10. Repeat step 9 with the 0.5 M, 0.75 M, 1.0 M, and unknown cuvettes.

11. Empty your samples into the appropriate waste container as specified by your teacher.

Data Table 1			
Molarity of solution (M_1)	**Volume of solution (V_1)**	**Molarity of stock solution (M_2)**	**Volume of stock solution (V_2)**
0.25 M	10 mL	1.0 M	
0.5 M	10 mL	1.0 M	
0.75 M	10 mL	1.0 M	

Data Table 2	
Sample	**% Absorbance**
0 M CuSO$_4$	0.0
0.25 M CuSO$_4$	
0.5 M CuSO$_4$	
0.75 M CuSO$_4$	
1.0 M CuSO$_4$	
Unknown	

Analysis

1. Describe the appearance of the five solutions you will test in this experiment.

2. Which solution do you think will have the lowest light absorbance? The highest? Why?

3. Why was it necessary to use a "blank" cuvette containing only distilled water in this experiment?

4. Graph the results of this lab using the information from Data Table 2. The molarity is the dependent variable (X-axis) and the absorbance is the independent variable (Y-axis). Plot the molarity versus absorbance for the known solutions using dots, and then connect them with lines.

5. How is the molarity of copper (II) sulfate related to the absorbance of light that passes through it?

6. How do your results compare with your prediction in Analysis question 2? Were the results as you expected?

7. Using the line created from your known data on your graph, plot the absorbance of the unknown solution and determine the molarity based on its location on the line graph. What was the molarity of the unknown solution?

8. What are some sources of error in this experiment that could have caused your results to be different than they should have been?

What's Going On?

Copper (II) sulfate is a gray compound that turns blue when it is hydrated. Concentrated solutions of $CuSO_4$ have a darker blue color than dilute solutions. Blue substances appear blue because they reflect blue light but absorb all other colors within the *visible spectrum* (see Figure 3). Blue solutions such as copper (II) sulfate most readily absorb orange light, which ranges from 585 to 620 nm. When analyzed using a spectrophotometer set to a wavelength within this range, the darker solutions absorb more of the light than the pale ones. Since the absorbance was set to 0 percent with pure water, as the concentration of the $CuSO_4$ increased, the amount of light absorbance increased as well. Impurities in the solution as well as smudges on the cuvettes can cause the readings to be different from those that are expected.

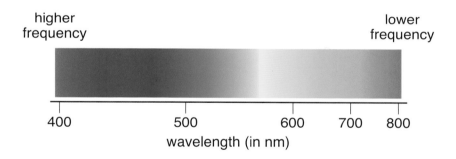

Figure 3

Visible spectrum

Connections

Spectrophotometry is frequently used for analytical purposes. Since the wavelength can be adjusted within a large range, a spectrophotometer can be calibrated to analyze a wide range of solutions. Spectrophotometric analysis can reveal the purity of medications and the concentrations of compounds within those medications. For example, the percentage of aspirin in over-the-counter aspirin tablets can be analyzed due to the reaction that aspirin has with iron (III) ion to produce an orange color. Spectrophotometry can also be used to analyze samples that absorb light outside of the visible spectrum, such as DNA and RNA. Since

DNA and RNA nucleotides absorb large amounts of ultraviolet light, the concentration of nucleic acids within a sample can be analyzed based on the absorbance of light in the 260-to-280 nm range.

Want to Know More?

See appendix for Our Findings.

Further Reading

Olson, John. "Determining Concentration using a Spectrophotometer." Available online. URL: http://www.ahs.stpaul.k12.mn.us/jolson/ chemistry/spec.html. Accessed July 17, 2010. Olson, of Arlington High School, St. Paul, Minnesota, explains how a spectrophotometer works on this Web page.

"Spectroscopy Fact Sheet: How Astronomers Study Light." Exploring Our Universe: From the Classroom to Outer Space. Available online. URL: http://fuse.pha.jhu.edu/outreach/kit1/factsheet.html. Accessed July 17, 2010. This resource, part of the FUSE (Far Ultraviolet Spectroscopic Explorer) Project's Public Outreach and Education program, discusses characteristics of visible light and the way these characteristics are studied with spectroscopy.

Volland, Walt. "Spectroscopy Lab." Available online. URL: http://www. trschools.com/staff/g/cgirtain/Weblabs/spectrolab.htm. Accessed July 17, 2010. On this Web page, Volland discusses the visible spectrum and explains how spectroscopy works.

12. Endothermic and Exothermic Reactions

Topic

Endothermic and exothermic reactions release or absorb heat as they occur.

Introduction

In all phases of matter, atoms are in constant motion. Atoms in gases have a free range of motion because the particles are spread very far apart. Therefore, the particles in a gas have a large amount of *kinetic energy*, the energy of motion. Particles in a liquid have less kinetic energy than gases, but more than solids. The atoms in a solid are moving, but they are locked into a structure that will not allow them to do more than just vibrate in place (Figure 1). As any type of particle moves, it gives off energy in the form of *heat*. The more kinetic energy a particle has the more heat it will give off to its surroundings; that heat can be measured as a change in *temperature*.

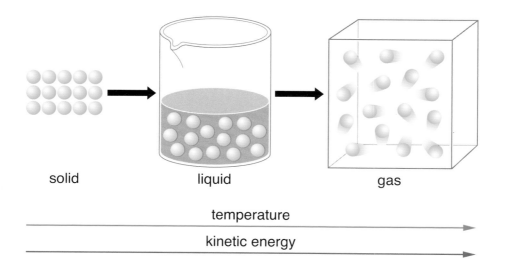

Figure 1

The movement of particles in solids, liquids, and gases

When a chemical reaction releases energy to its environment the temperature of the environment rises. Such reactions are described as *exothermic*. In exothermic reactions, heat is released when particle movement slows and when high-energy bonds between atoms are broken. Therefore, water freezing to form ice and combustion reactions are both examples of exothermic reactions. The opposite of exothermic reactions are *endothermic reactions*, which absorb energy from their environment. In an endothermic reaction such as the melting of ice, the surrounding environment loses heat. Chemical reactions that do not occur without the addition of energy are endothermic. In this experiment, you will perform endothermic and exothermic reactions, monitor the changes in temperature that occurs in the surrounding environment, and plot your results on a graph.

Time Required

25 minutes for Part A
25 minutes for Part B

Materials

- barium hydroxide octahydrate (solid)
- ammonium chloride (solid)
- magnesium metal strips
- 6 molar (M) hydrochloric acid
- baking soda
- 2 beakers (about 250 milliliters [ml])
- electronic balance
- disposable weigh boats
- small block of wood (slightly larger than the diameter of the beaker)
- stirring rod
- wash bottle filled with distilled water
- Celsius (C) thermometer
- hot mitts
- goggles

    ➥   scissors

    ➥   science notebook

Safety Note   Goggles must be worn at all times during this experiment. Use extreme caution with the chemicals used in this lab. Perform the experiment in a fume hood if possible and *never* directly sniff the beakers. Please review and follow the safety guidelines at the beginning of this volume.

Procedure, Part A: Endothermic Reaction

1. Copy Data Tables 1 and 2 into your science notebook. Leave room to extend beyond 6 minutes.

2. Measure out 17 grams (g) of ammonium chloride and 32 g of barium hydroxide octahydrate into separate weigh boats.

3. Place a block of wood flat on your lab table. Wet the entire top surface of the wood using a wash bottle. Wet the bottom and sides of a beaker, then place it on top the block of wood.

4. Pour the barium hydroxide powder into the beaker. Measure the temperature of the beaker containing the solid. Record this as your initial temperature (0 minutes [min]) on Data Table 1.

5. Add the solid ammonium chloride to the beaker and stir to mix.

6. While keeping the beaker on the block of wet wood, stir the contents of the beaker and record the temperature every 60 seconds (sec) until the temperature remains constant for two readings. Record each temperature reading on Data Table 1.

7. Lift the beaker and observe. The mixture should have become cold enough to freeze the beaker to the block of wood.

8. The contents of the beaker can be safely washed down the sink with water.

Procedure, Part B: Exothermic Reaction

1. Add approximately 50 ml of 6M hydrochloric acid to a beaker. Place a thermometer in the beaker and record the initial temperature (0 min) on Data Table 2.

2. Cut a 4-inch (in.) (10.2-centimeter [cm]) piece of magnesium ribbon into small pieces (about 0.25 in. [0.6 cm] long).

3. Add the magnesium ribbon pieces to the hydrochloric acid and stir to mix.

4. Record the temperature every 60 sec until the temperature remains constant for two readings. Record each temperature reading on Data Table 2.

5. Neutralize the solution by adding baking soda to the beaker until bubbling ceases. Wash the contents of the beaker down the drain.

Data Table 1	
Time (min)	Temperature (°C)
0	
1	
2	
3	
4	
5	
6	

Data Table 2	
Time (min)	Temperature (°C)
0	
1	
2	
3	
4	
5	
6	

Analysis

1. The reaction between barium hydroxide and ammonium chloride forms ammonia gas, aqueous barium chloride, and liquid water. Write the balanced chemical equation that occurs in this reaction.

2. Describe the visible evidence that a reaction was occurring between the barium chloride and ammonium chloride.

3. Graph the temperature changes that occurred over time in the endothermic reaction as a line graph.

4. The reaction between magnesium metal and aqueous hydrochloric acid forms hydrogen gas and aqueous magnesium chloride. Write the balanced chemical equation for the reaction that occurs.

5. How could you tell that a reaction was occurring between the magnesium and hydrochloric acid?

6. Graph the temperature changes that occurred over time in the exothermic reaction as a line graph.

7. Compare the graphs of the endothermic and exothermic reactions. How are the two graphs different?

What's Going On?

All chemical reactions require a certain amount of *activation energy* to begin the reaction process. Endothermic reactions require more activation energy to get started than exothermic ones do. As a result, endothermic reactions absorb heat energy from their environment to drive the reaction forward. Figure 2 shows the amount of energy needed to begin an endothermic reaction. A large amount of energy is required for the reactants to form the *activated complex*, which will react and result in the products formed in the reaction. After the initial energy, known as the activation energy (E_a), is reached the reaction proceeds spontaneously and will generally release a small amount of energy. However, the small amount of energy given off in an endothermic reaction is not enough to compensate for the extra energy required to start the reaction, and there is still a marked temperature difference in the environment, noted as ΔH, or the change in heat experienced in the environment. As the reaction proceeds, the temperature of the surrounding environment decreases because the heat is transferred from the surroundings to the reactants. When barium hydroxide and ammonium chloride react, the reaction needs so much energy that the temperature of the surrounding environment drops below the freezing point of water.

In an exothermic reaction, the amount of activation energy needed is much lower than in an endothermic one. These reactions may initially absorb a small amount of heat, but as the reaction progresses, a much greater amount of energy is given off in the form of heat. In Figure 3, you can see that the amount of activation energy (E_a) needed to form the activated complex is much lower than in an endothermic reaction. After the activated complex is formed, the formation of products occurs spontaneously and a large amount of energy is released. Even though a small amount of energy is used to begin the reaction, a great deal more energy is released than was needed as activation energy. The additional energy released is given off as heat, indicated by ΔH. Exothermic reactions release a large amount of energy due to the breaking of high-energy bonds between atoms or the increase in kinetic energy of the products. In the reaction between magnesium metal and hydrochloric acid, the metal ionizes and forms an aqueous solution and chloride ions from the acid. The hydrogen from the aqueous acid solution is released as a gas. Since the products have more kinetic energy than the reactants, energy is released in the form of heat.

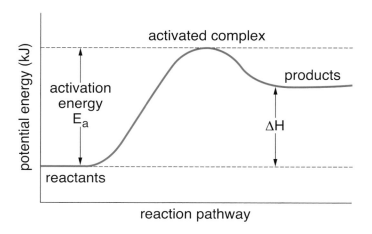

Figure 2

Endothermic reaction

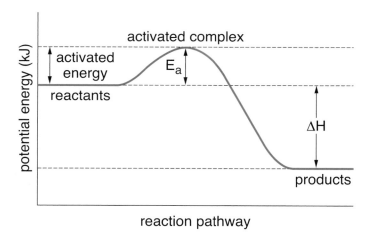

Figure 3

Exothermic reaction

Connections

In exothermic reactions, the release of a large amount of energy occurs all at once. For example, in the combustion of a hydrocarbon, the energy is discharged in one large explosion. You might see this type of reaction if an entire container of *octane*, the hydrocarbon in gasoline, were set on fire. The container would erupt into a large flame that releases heat in a huge burst into the environment. However, if that same container of gasoline is put into a *combustion engine* of an automobile, the energy is released slowly in smaller steps. In a combustion engine, small amounts of gasoline are ignited in enclosed cylinders within the engine. As a result, the quantity of energy released is controlled. Energy is still given off as heat, but it is much more efficient than a large explosion that would have occurred if the gasoline were simply to go through one large combustion reaction. In this way, the energy released by breaking the bonds in the hydrocarbon can be used to do work.

Want to Know More?

See appendix for Our Findings.

Further Reading

"Endothermic and Exothermic Processes." Mr. Kent's Chemistry Page. Available online. URL: http://www.kentchemistry.com/links/Matter/ EndoExo.htm. Accessed July 17, 2010. Two short video clips on this Web page demonstrate endothermic and exothormic reactions.

"Energy Diagrams." Mr. Guch's Cavalcade O'Chemistry. Available online. URL: http://misterguch.brinkster.net/energydiagram.html. Accessed July 17, 2010. Mr. Guch, a chemistry teacher, explains the transfer of energy during a chemical reaction on this Web page.

Jones, Larry. "Endothermic vs. Exothermic Reactions," June 27, 2009. Pickens County School District. http://www.sciencebyjones.com/ endoexothermic.htm. Accessed July 17, 2010. On his school Web site, Larry Jones provides concise, easy-to-understand explanations of endothermic and exothermic chemical reactions.

13. Finding Molar Mass

Topic

The ideal gas law can be used to determine the molar mass of butane.

Introduction

Gases behave differently from solids or liquids because their particles move very rapidly and are spread far apart. Gases take the shape of any container that they occupy. They can be pressurized by adding more particles or increasing the temperature inside of a fixed-volume container. All gases have similar characteristics; therefore, all gases behave in a fairly predictable manner. The pressure, volume, number of moles, and temperature of a gas are all related. Any one of these variables can be determined when the others are known using the *ideal gas* equation:

$$PV = nRT$$

in which P represents pressure, measured in either atmospheres (atm) or kilopascals (kPa); V represents volume in liters; n stands for the number of mol of a gas; and T is the temperature in Kelvins (K). R is the ideal gas constant, which is either

$$0.0821 \text{ L} \times \frac{atm}{mol} \times K \quad \text{or} \quad 8.31 \text{ L} \times \frac{kPa}{mol} \times K,$$

depending on the units that were used to measure the pressure.

The ideal gas equation is very versatile and can be rearranged to solve for any of the variables in it. In this experiment, you will measure the pressure, volume, and temperature of *butane*, the gas found in disposable lighters (Figure 1). From this data, you determine the number of moles of butane and the mass of butane collected during the experiment along with the molar mass of butane.

Time Required

45 minutes

Figure 1
Disposable butane lighter

Materials

- disposable butane lighter
- hair dryer
- electronic balance
- 50-milliliter (ml) graduated cylinder
- plastic container or trough for holding water (at least 12 inches [in.] [30 centimeters (cm)] deep)
- access to water
- barometer
- vapor pressure table
- Celsius (C) thermometer
- periodic table of elements (see page 175)
- science notebook

> **Safety Note**   Be careful when handling the lighter. Please review and follow the safety guidelines at the beginning of this volume.

Procedure

1. Find the mass of a disposable butane lighter to the nearest 0.01 gram (g). Record the mass on the first row of Data Table 1.

2. Fill a large plastic container with room temperature water. Find the temperature of the water using a thermometer. Record the temperature on Data Table 1.

3. Remove the plastic base from a 50-ml graduated cylinder so that you can see the bottom of it. Immerse the graduated cylinder under the water in the large container, filling it with water. Keeping the mouth of the graduated cylinder underwater, invert it. Check to make sure that no air bubbles are trapped in the cylinder.

4. Hold the lighter in one hand and the graduated cylinder in the other (or have a partner hold the cylinder for you). Lift the cylinder slightly and place the lighter in the water directly beneath the graduated cylinder.

5. Carefully release butane from the lighter by pressing the button that controls the gas valve until the gas fills the cylinder to nearly 45 ml. Remove the lighter and set the mouth of the graduated cylinder down on the bottom of the container, inverted, for 2 to 3 minutes (min).

6. Move the graduated cylinder so that the waterline inside the cylinder is even with the waterline in the plastic container (this ensures that the pressure is equal to atmospheric pressure) and measure the exact volume of gas collected in the graduated cylinder. Record this measurement on Data Table 1.

7. Use a hair dryer to dry the lighter completely (about 3 to 5 min). Once the water has been dried off, find the mass of the lighter. Record the mass on the second row of Data Table 1.

8. Take a barometric pressure reading from the barometer and record it on the data table.

Analysis

1. Calculate the mass of butane used by subtracting the mass of the lighter after releasing the butane from the initial mass. Record the mass on Data Table 1.

Data Table 1	
Mass of lighter before butane is released	
Mass of lighter after butane is released	
Mass of butane (lighter mass before minus lighter mass after)	
Temperature (°C) of water	
Volume of butane (ml)	
Barometric pressure	
Pressure of butane (barometric pressure minus partial pressure of water vapor)	

2. Which of the following values for the gas constant (R) will you use:

$$0.0821 \text{ L} \times \frac{\text{atm}}{\text{mol}} \times \text{K} \quad or \quad 8.31 \text{ L} \times \frac{\text{kPa}}{\text{mol}} \times \text{K}?$$

(*Hint*: look at the units in your barometric pressure reading.)

3. Using the temperature of the water from Data Table 1, find the partial pressure of water vapor in your experiment on Data Table 2, which shows how water vapor pressure varies as temperature increases. Use the value from Data Table 2 as well as the barometric pressure to determine the partial pressure of butane using the following equation (*Dalton's law of partial pressure*):

$$P_{total} = P_1 + P_2$$

where P_{total} is the barometric pressure, P_1 is the vapor pressure of water, and P_2 is the pressure of butane.

4. Convert the volume measurement from Data Table 1 from milliliters to liters by dividing by 1,000.

Data Table 2 Water Vapor Pressure Table					
Temperature (°C)	Pressure (mmHg)	Temperature (°C)	Pressure (mmHg)	Temperature (°C)	Pressure (mmHg)
0.0	4.6	19.5	17.0	27.0	26.7
5.0	6.5	20.0	17.5	28.0	28.3
10.0	9.2	20.5	18.1	29.0	30.0
12.5	10.9	21.0	18.6	30.0	31.8
15.0	12.8	21.5	19.2	35.0	42.2
15.5	13.2	22.0	19.8	40.0	55.3
16.0	13.6	22.5	20.4	50.0	92.5
16.5	14.1	23.0	21.1	60.0	149.4
17.0	14.5	23.5	21.7	70.0	233.7
17.5	15.0	24.0	22.4	80.0	355.1
18.0	15.5	24.5	23.1	90.0	525.8
18.5	16.0	25.0	23.8	95.0	633.9
19.0	16.5	26.0	25.2	100.0	760.0

Note: for conversions: 1 atm = 760 mmHg = 101.325 kPa

5. Convert the temperature from Data Table 1 to K (°C + 273).

6. Use the information that you have to calculate the moles of butane, using the ideal gas equation, $PV = nRT$, which can be rearranged to:

$$n = \frac{PV}{RT}$$

where n = moles.

7. Use the moles of butane and the mass of butane from the data table to calculate the experimental molar (m) mass of butane using the equation:

$$M = \frac{m}{n}$$

where M = molar mass, m = mass, and n = moles.

8. The formula for butane is C_4H_{10}. Using the periodic table of the elements, calculate the molar mass of butane.

9. Determine the percent error for your calculated value using the equation:

experimental value − actual value/actual value × 100 percent.

10. How close was your calculated value to the actual molar mass of butane? What were some sources of error that could have caused the results to be different from what was expected?

What's Going On?

The chemical formula for butane is C_4H_{10} and the actual molar mass of butane is 58.12 g/mol. Figure 2 shows the structural formula of butane. In this experiment, the butane was collected in a graduated cylinder that was held under water to ensure that the gas was not lost to the atmosphere. The volume was measured at the surface of the water to ensure that the atmospheric pressure was equal to the combination of gases within the graduated cylinder, which included butane and some water vapor that was present due to evaporation. For this reason, Dalton's law was used to calculate the pressure of butane. The pressure, volume, and temperature can all be used to calculate the number of moles of butane collected. Since the number of moles of a substance is equal to its mass divided by its molar mass, the moles of butane and the mass obtained from weighing the lighter before and after collection could be used to determine the experimental molar mass of butane.

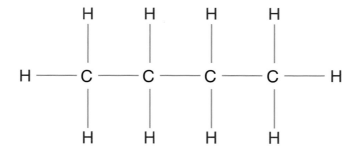

Figure 2

Structural formula for butane

Connections

The ideal gas equation was established as a combination of several existing gas laws. *Boyle's law* ($P_1V_1 = P_2V_2$) shows the relationship between pressure and volume. Charles' law ($V_1/T_1 = V_2/T_2$) shows the relationship between volume and temperature. Avogadro's law ($V_1/n_1 = V_2/n_2$) discusses the relationship between the volume of a gas and the number of moles, and Gay-Lussac's law ($P_1/T_1 = P_2/T_2$) shows the relationship between pressure and temperature. All of these laws are expressed in the combined gas law, $P_1V_1/T_1 = P_2V_2/T_2$. The pressure of a combination of gases can be determined using Dalton's law of partial pressures ($P_{total} = P_1 + P_2 + P_3$. . .), where the partial pressures of all gases can be added together to equal the total pressure of a gas.

The ideal gas law ties in the relationship between temperature, pressure, volume, and the number of moles of gas in a closed system. However, for a gas to be considered an "ideal gas" that can be calculated by this equation, it must follow the rules of the kinetic theory. The kinetic theory has five parts:

1. Gas molecules are in constant, random motion.
2. Most of the volume of a gas is empty space and the volume of the molecules is negligible.
3. The molecules of a gas experience no forces of attraction or repulsion.
4. The impact of gas molecules is completely elastic and therefore no energy is lost in collision between molecules.
5. The temperature of a gas is equal to the kinetic energy of all its molecules.

Under normal conditions, the ideal gas law is reasonably accurate. However, when a gas is near its *condensation point*, its *critical point*, or is highly pressurized, the ideal gas equation will not be accurate. In such cases, a real-gas equation such as the van der Waals gas equation (Figure 3), which accounts for attractive forces, can be used.

$$(p + \frac{a \cdot n^2}{V^2})(v - n \cdot b) = n \cdot R \cdot T$$

where:
p = pressure
V = volume
T = temperature
R = gas content
a and b = specific constants
for each gas

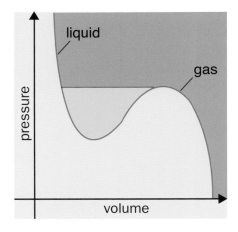

Figure 3

Van der Waals equation for real gas and a graph of the equation

Want to Know More?

See appendix for Our Findings.

Further Reading

Blauch, David N. "Gas Laws," 2009. Virtual Chemistry. Available online. URL: http://www.chm.davidson.edu/vce/gaslaws/. Accessed July 17, 2010. Blauch provides an interactive page where students can change the pressure or temperature of a gas to see how volume is affected.

"Gas Laws." UNC–Chapel Hill Chemistry Fundamentals Program, 2008. Available online. URL: http://www.shodor.net/UNChem/advanced/gas/index.html. Accessed July 17, 2010. This Web page discusses the characteristics and behavior of gases and relates these to the gas laws.

Nave, C. R. "Ideal Gas Law." Hyperphysics, 2005. Available online. URL: http://hyperphysics.phy-astr.gsu.edu/HBASE/kinetic/idegas.html. Accessed on July 17, 2010. Hosted by the Department of Physics and Astronomy, Georgia State University, Hyperphysics explains many basic concepts in science, including the Ideal Gas Law.

14. Chemical Moles

Topic

In the conversion of baking soda to table salt, the ratio of moles of reactant to moles of product can be calculated.

Introduction

Chemical equations show the reactants and products of a chemical reaction. Chemical equations must be balanced to show that matter is not gained or lost in a reaction. Therefore, the amounts of each type of atom must be the same on both the *reactant* and *product* sides of the equation. A balanced chemical equation includes *coefficients* that show the mole ratio, ratio of reactants and products to each other. For example, in the chemical equation

$$2\ Mg + O_2 \rightarrow 2\ MgO$$

the coefficients show that the reaction requires 2 moles of magnesium for every 1 mole of oxygen gas to form 2 moles of magnesium oxide.

By using mole ratios and the amount of one reactant or product, the amount of the other reactant or product in a chemical reaction can be calculated. In this experiment, you will determine how many grams (g) of sodium chloride, or table salt, will be produced from the reaction of a precise amount of baking soda with an excess amount of hydrochloric acid (see Figure 1). Then you will perform the reaction, isolate sodium chloride, and determine the percent yield of your reaction.

Time Required

45 minutes

Materials

- baking soda (sodium bicarbonate), about 2 g
- 6 molars (M) hydrochloric acid

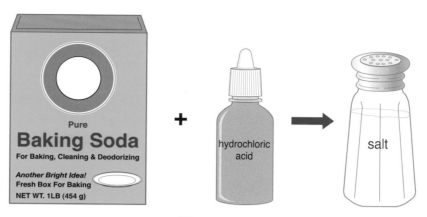

Figure 1

When baking soda reacts with hydrochloric acid, table salt is produced

- medium (250-to-400 milliliter [ml]) beaker
- electronic balance
- graduated cylinder
- scoopula
- ring stand
- ring clamp
- wire gauze
- Bunsen burner
- flint sparker
- stirring rod
- watch glass (diameter of beaker or larger)
- calculator
- hot mitts
- goggles
- periodic table of elements (see page 175)
- science notebook

Safety Note   Goggles must be worn at all times during this experiment. Use caution when using strong acids and while heating over an open flame. Perform this experiment under a fume hood or in a well-ventilated area as dangerous vapors will be produced. Please review and follow the safety guidelines at the beginning of this volume.

Procedure

1. Find the mass of a beaker with a watch glass "lid." Record the mass of both items together to the nearest 0.01 gram (g) on the data table.

2. Remove the watch glass from the beaker, zero the balance, and add approximately 2.00 g of baking soda to the beaker. Record the exact mass to the nearest 0.01 g on the data table.

3. Measure 5 to 6 ml of 6 M hydrochloric acid into a graduated cylinder. The exact amount is not important, as this reagent is in excess.

4. Slowly and carefully add the hydrochloric acid to the beaker of baking soda. The mixture will bubble rapidly and the beaker will be very hot.

5. After the intense bubbling has slowed, stir the mixture with a stirring rod until the bubbling ceases.

6. Set up a ring clamp on a ring stand and place a piece of wire gauze on the ring to serve as a base for the beaker to sit on (Figure 2). Position the Bunsen burner under the wire gauze.

7. Place the beaker on top of the ring apparatus and place the watch glass over the top of the beaker to prevent splattering.

8. Light the Bunsen burner using a flint sparker and adjust the flame so that it is nearly touching the bottom of the beaker on the ring apparatus.

9. Heat the mixture in the beaker until all the liquid has evaporated.

10. Allow the beaker and its contents to cool for about 5 minutes.

11. Find the mass of the beaker, watch glass, and all of its contents to the nearest 0.01 g. Record the mass on the data table.

12. The material in the beaker is table salt, which can be thrown in the trash can or dissolved in water and washed down the sink when you clean up.

Analysis

1. Write the complete balanced equation that occurs between baking soda ($NaHCO_3$) and hydrochloric acid (HCl) to form sodium chloride (NaCl), water (H_2O), and carbon dioxide (CO_2).

2. What is the mole ratio of baking soda to sodium chloride?

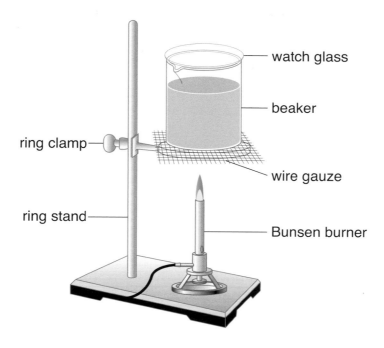

watch glass

beaker

ring clamp

wire gauze

ring stand

Bunsen burner

Figure 2

Place the beaker on a ring stand above a Bunsen burner.

Data Table	
Measurement	**Mass (g)**
Mass of beaker and watch glass	
Mass of baking soda	
Mass of beaker, watch glass, and contents	
Mass of salt (total mass minus beaker and lid)	

3. Using the periodic table of elements, find the M mass of both baking soda and salt.

4. Use the exact mass of baking soda recorded on the data table and the M mass of baking soda to calculate the moles of baking soda that were used in this experiment.

5. Use the moles from Analysis question 4 and the mole ratio for baking soda to sodium chloride to calculate the moles of salt that should be produced.

6. Use the moles of salt from Analysis question 5 and the molar mass of salt (sodium chloride) to determine the expected mass of salt produced.

7. Calculate the percent yield for this reaction using the actual yield of salt measured (from the data table) and the theoretical yield from Analysis question 6. The formula for this calculation is:

$$\text{percent yield} = \frac{\text{actual yield}}{\text{theoretical yield}} \times 100 \text{ percent}$$

8. Describe some factors that may have caused your percent yield to be low in this experiment.

What's Going On?

Hydrochloric acid is a strong acid and baking soda is a weak base. The reaction between any acid and base, a *neutralization reaction*, always produces a type of salt and water. In the neutralization that occurs between baking soda and hydrochloric acid, the products are sodium chloride, water, and carbon dioxide. Since the sodium chloride is the only solid product of this reaction, simply evaporating all of the water off of the product can isolate it.

If the amount of one of the reactants in this chemical reaction is known, the theoretical yield of any of the products can be determined by using the balanced chemical equation and the mole ratio. However, since chemical reactions rarely occur under perfect conditions, theoretical yields are not always obtained. In order to assess how close the actual results from an experiment are to the theoretical yield, a percent yield can be calculated. Percent yields can be greater than or less than 100 percent depending on whether the actual yield was higher or lower than the theoretical yield. The closer the yield is to 100 percent, the more accurate it is.

Connections

Baking soda is a very useful product both in the chemistry laboratory and in a home. As a weak base, it can neutralize dangerous acid spills in a chemistry laboratory so that they can be cleaned up safely. Baking soda can also be ingested as an antacid to neutralize the hydrochloric acid in the stomach. In the kitchen, baking soda helps dough to rise when making breads and pastries, so it is commonly added to recipes. It can also be used as a multipurpose cleaner and even as a toothpaste and breath freshener. In the refrigerator, baking soda absorbs odors and keep foods smelling fresh. It can be sprinkled on carpets and upholstery to absorb unpleasant odors as well. Baking soda is also helpful to keep around in case of fire emergencies, as it will cut off the oxygen to grease and electrical fires and put them out.

Want to Know More?

See appendix for Our Findings.

Further Reading

Bailey, Kristy M. "Stoichiometry Tutorial: Finding and Using Molar Ratios." Available online. URL: http://www.occc.edu/KMBailey/Chem1115Tutorials/Molar_Ratios.htm. Accessed July 17, 2010. Dr. Bailey, of Oklahoma City Community College, explains how to find molar ratios and provides sample problems.

MHS Chemistry, "Moles and Mole Ratios," January 30, 2008. Available online. URL: http://www.dbooth.net/mhs/chem/moles.html. Accessed July 17, 2010. Mr. Zahm, of Middletown High School in Rhode Island, provides a thorough explanation of the use of mole ratios in chemistry.

"Stoichiometry." UNC–Chapel Hill Chemistry Fundamentals Program, 2008. Available online. URL: http://shodor.com/UNChem/basic/stoic/index.html. Accessed July 17, 2010. This Web page explains the use of mol measurements in chemistry and equation writing, and includes some sample problems and solutions.

15. Heat Energy

Topic

The amount of heat released per mole of three different fuels can be determined experimentally.

Introduction

Chemical bonds contain energy. When the bonds between atoms are broken, energy is released. Work can be accomplished by releasing the energy in small, controlled steps. However, if all the energy is released at one time, as in a *combustion reaction*, most of that energy is given off to the surroundings as heat. The amount of heat given off in a combustion reaction varies depending on the number of bonds and the types of atoms in those bonds. The heat of combustion for a substance can be determined experimentally by measuring the temperature change of the environment when a fuel is burned. The equation to determine the amount of heat of a substance is

$$q = m\, C\, \Delta T$$

where q represents the amount of heat in joules (J), m is the mass of the substance in grams (g), C is the *specific heat* constant for that particular substance, and ΔT is the temperature change in degree Celsius (°C) or Kelvin (K).

In this experiment, you will burn three different fuels and determine their heat of combustion by measuring the temperature change in a beaker of water. After the heat transferred to the water is calculated, you will determine the amount of heat given off per mole of each substance and compare your experimental values with the actual values for each fuel tested.

 **Time Required**

45 minutes

Materials

- ring stand
- ring clamp
- beaker (the same diameter as the ring so that the beaker can fit into the ring and be held in place by the rim of the beaker)
- graduated cylinder
- cold water (300 milliliters [ml])
- Celsius (C) thermometer
- small piece of Styrofoam™ (about 1/4 to 1/2 inch [in.] [0.63 to 1.27 centimeters (cm)] thick and large enough to cover the mouth of the beaker)
- knife
- masking tape
- 3 spirit burners
- matches
- methanol (CH_3OH) (enough to fill a small spirit burner one-quarter full)
- ethanol (C_2H_5OH) (enough to fill a small spirit burner one-quarter full)
- propanol ($CH_3CH_2CH_2OH$) (enough to fill a small spirit burner one-quarter full)
- isopropanol ($(CH_3)_2CH_2OH$) (enough to fill a small spirit burner one-quarter full)
- butanol (C_4H_9OH) (enough to fill a small spirit burner one-quarter full)
- electronic balance
- aluminum foil
- hot mitts
- goggles
- access to chemistry textbook or Internet
- science notebook

Safety Note Goggles must be worn at all times during this experiment. Use caution with flames and combustible fuels. Please review and follow the safety guidelines at the beginning of this volume.

Procedure

1. Fill a beaker with 100 ml of cold water.

2. Create a lid for the beaker by cutting a piece of Styrofoam™ that is large enough to cover the entire top of the beaker.

3. Carefully push a thermometer through the center of your Styrofoam™ lid so that the tip will be fully immersed in the water but will not touch the bottom or side of the beaker. Tape the thermometer in place.

4. Set up a ring clamp on the ring stand. Place the beaker with lid and thermometer into the ring (see Figure 1).

5. Position a spirit burner directly beneath the beaker so that the flame will slightly touch the bottom of the beaker when it is lit.

6. Wrap the apparatus (beaker and burner) with several layers of aluminum foil to insulate it. Leave some small air holes so that oxygen will be available for the combustion process. Arrange the aluminum foil with a flap or door that will enable you exchange the spirit burners and refill the beaker of water between trials.

7. Choose an alcohol from the available selection of fuels. Fill the spirit burner about one-quarter full of the chosen fuel.

8. Use the electronic balance to find the initial mass of the spirit burner and fuel and record the mass on Data Table 1.

9. Record the initial temperature of the water (shown on the thermometer) in the beaker on Data Table 1.

10. Position the spirit burner underneath the beaker. Use matches to light the wick of the burner. Quickly replace the insulating layers of aluminum foil so that no heat will be lost.

11. Allow the fuel to burn and heat the water in the beaker. Monitor the temperature of the water until it remains stable for 1 minute (min). Record the final temperature on Data Table 1.

12. Extinguish the spirit burner and allow it to cool. Find the final mass of the spirit burner and record it on Data Table 1.

13. Replace the water in the beaker with 100 ml of cold water. Repeat steps 7 through 12 with two more fuels.

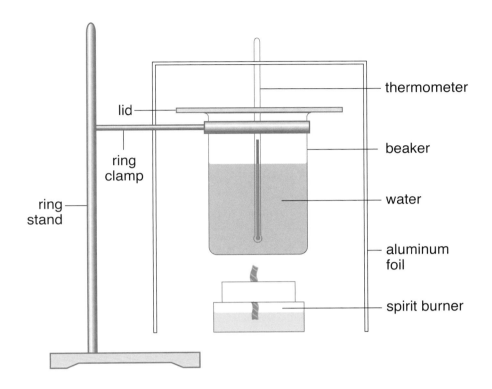

Figure 1

Data Table 1			
	Trial 1 Fuel = _____	**Trial 2 Fuel =** _____	**Trial 3 Fuel =** _____
Initial mass of spirit burner			
Final mass of spirit burner			
Initial temperature of water			
Final temperature of water			

Analysis

1. Write the molecular formula for each fuel on Data Table 2. Calculate the molar (M) mass for each of the three fuels, using the molecular formulas. Record the M mass on Data Table 2.

2. Subtract the final mass of each spirit burner from its initial mass in order to calculate the mass of fuel used for each of the three trials and record them on Data Table 2.

3. Use the mass of each of the three fuels used and each fuel's molar mass to calculate the mol of fuel used:

$$\text{moles} = \frac{\text{mass}}{\text{M mass}}$$

   Record the moles on Data Table 2.

4. Calculate the change in temperature that occurred in each of the three trials (final temperature − initial temperature) and record it on Data Table 2.

5. For this laboratory, we will assume that all of the energy from the combustion of the fuel was absorbed by the water. Therefore, the amount of energy gained by the water will be equal to the heat of combustion for the fuel. Calculate the heat of the reaction for each of the three fuels using the equation $q = m\,C\,\Delta T$, where

   q = heat energy

   m = mass of water (assume that 1 ml of water weighs 1 g)

   C = specific heat of water (4.184 joules (J)/g°C)

   ΔT = change in temperature in °C

6. Convert the heat of each reaction from joules to kilojoules (kJ) by dividing by 1,000.

7. Calculate the amount of heat per mole of each substance by dividing the heat of reaction by the moles of fuel (from Analysis question 3). The units for the heat of combustion will be in kJ/mol.

8. Which fuel had the highest heat of combustion? What characteristics of this fuel do you think caused it to release more energy than the others?

9. Look up the actual heat of combustion for each of the fuels you used in this experiment. Calculate your percent error:

$$\text{actual value} - \frac{\text{experimental value} - \text{actual value}}{\text{actual value}} \times 100\%$$

10. What were some sources of error in this experiment that could have increased your percent error?

Data Table 2			
	Fuel 1	**Fuel 2**	**Fuel 3**
Molecular formula			
M mass			
Mass used			
Moles of fuel used (mass/M mass)			
Temperature change			
Heat of reaction			
Heat in kJ			
Heat per mol			

What's Going On?

When energy is released as heat, it is transferred to the surrounding environment. In this experiment, combustion of each fuel increased the temperature of the water in the beaker above the spirit burner. Therefore, the mass of the water, its temperature change, and its specific heat could be used to calculate the heat of the reaction. For the calculations in this laboratory, it was assumed that all of the heat released from the fuels was transferred to the water. However, even though the apparatus was insulated, it is inevitable that some heat was lost to the outside environment. Therefore, the calculated heat of combustion for each substance was most likely lower than the actual value.

Bonds between atoms contain energy that is released when those bonds are broken. The heat released per mole of a substance largely depends on the number and the strength of those bonds. In this experiment, alcohols were burned. Alcohols consist of chains of carbon with a hydroxyl group at one end (see Figure 2). Carbon atoms form strong, covalent bonds that contain a lot of energy. Therefore, fuels made of bonded carbon tend to release a large amount of heat when they are burned. The amount of heat increases when the size of the molecule increases.

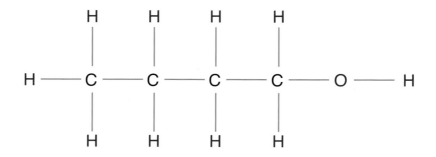

Figure 2

Structure of an alcohol

Connections

The heat of combustion for a substance can be measured much more accurately than in this experiment by using a *bomb calorimeter*. Such a calorimeter is a closed, insulated device that holds a sample container, which is usually immersed in water (see Figure 3). A substance is placed into the sample well and the container is sealed. A switch ignites the substance in the sample well using electrodes, and a detector measures the temperature change of the water while the water is being continuously stirred. Because bomb calorimeters are highly insulated and often pressurized, they provide accurate readings of temperature change. Most bomb calorimeters digitally display the temperature changes. Some bomb calorimeters even contain a computerized output so that all of the calculations for the heat of combustion are completed by the device.

 ## Want to Know More?

See appendix for Our Findings.

Further Reading

Blauch, David N. "Calorimetry: Heat of Combustion of Methane," 2009. Available online. URL: http://www.chm.davidson.edu/vce/Calorimetry/

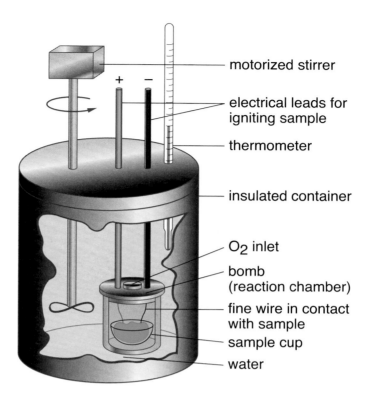

Figure 3

Bomb calorimeter

HeatOfCombustionofMethane.html. Accessed July 17, 2010. This interactive lesson simulates the combustion of methane in a bomb calorimeter.

Boggan, Bill. "Alcohol and You." General Chemistry Case Studies, 2003. Available online. URL: http://www.chemcases.com/alcohol/index.htm. Accessed July 17, 2010. Dr. Boggan, of Kennesaw State University in Georgia, explains the chemistry of several alcohols and discusses the effects of alcohol on the body.

"Calculating Heat of Combustion." 2010. Polymer Science Learning Center, University of Southern Mississippi. Available online. URL: http://pslc.ws/fire/cellulos/combcals.htm. Accessed July 17, 2010. This Web page shows how to calculate the heat of combustion for methane.

16. Chloride Levels

Topic

Levels of chloride ions in water samples can be measured.

Introduction

Do you ever wonder what is in your drinking water? Chances are, even if you are drinking water that has been purified and disinfected, it still contains traces of minerals and chemicals that were either obtained from the environment or added to the water to kill bacteria. Chloride ions are just one of several substances that are commonly found in water. The element chlorine occurs naturally in the environment in compounds or as chlorine gas. Chlorine is highly reactive in its natural state, so it generally forms *ionic bonds* with other atoms to create compounds. When ionic compounds such as sodium chloride (NaCl) dissolve in water, they break down into their respective *ions*, which in the case of sodium chloride are Na^+ and Cl^-. Figure 1 shows how individual ions are surrounded by water molecules and separated from each other. Chloride makes its way into waterways in two ways: from the natural breakdown of chloride-containing minerals and from the addition of chlorine to water as a disinfecting agent.

Generally, small doses of chloride in water are not considered harmful. Some people do not like the taste of chloride in their water, but it is fairly rare for individuals to suffer illness due to the intake of small amounts of this ion. However, large quantities of chloride can cause health problems. Some studies have shown that the presence of chloride ions correlates to disorders with the immune system, cardiovascular system, and respiratory system. Other research indicates that chloride ions, when combined with organic compounds that occur naturally in the environment, create substances that can cause cancer. Therefore, detecting and measuring chloride in water is important. In this experiment, you will test three different samples of water for the presence of chloride ions by titrating the samples with silver nitrate.

Time Required

60 minutes

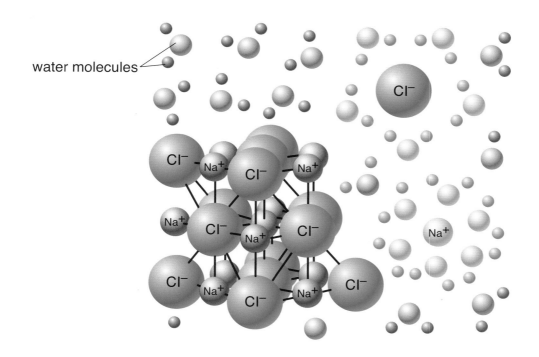

Figure 1

In water, sodium chlorides dissociate into sodium ions and chloride ions.

Materials

- burette
- ring stand
- burette clamp
- Erlenmeyer flask (100-milliliter [ml] size or larger)
- 3 100- to 200-ml beakers
- graduated cylinder
- stirring rod
- spatula
- 0.1 molar (M) silver nitrate ($AgNO_3$) standardized solution
- 5 percent potassium chromate (K_2CrO_4) solution
- pH test strips
- baking soda

➥   vinegar

➥   samples of water from 3 locations (such as tap water, groundwater, lake water, stream water, or rain water)

➥   apron

➥   goggles

➥   science notebook

Safety Note   Goggles must be worn at all times during this experiment. Use caution when working with chemicals. Silver nitrate can cause staining of the skin and clothing. Please review and follow the safety guidelines at the beginning of this volume.

Procedure

1. Label three beakers as 1, 2, and 3. Pour about 50 ml of water sample 1 into beaker 1, about 50 ml of water sample 2 into beaker 2, and about 50 ml of water sample 3 into beaker 3. On the data table, indicate the source of each water sample.

2. Answer Analysis question 1.

3. Test the pH of each water sample using pH paper. The pH of each sample must be between 7 and 10 to carry out a successful *titration*.

    ✔ If the pH is below 7, stir in baking soda, a little at a time, until the pH is in the correct range.

    ✔ If the pH is above 10, stir in vinegar, a little at a time, until the pH is in the correct range.

4. Set up a burette on a ring stand using a burette clamp (see Figure 2) and fill the burette with standardized silver nitrate.

5. Using a graduated cylinder, measure 10 ml of sample 1 from its beaker and pour it into an Erlenmeyer flask.

6. Add 3 to 4 drops of potassium chromate indicator to the sample in the flask.

7. Record the initial volume of silver nitrate in the burette on the data table.

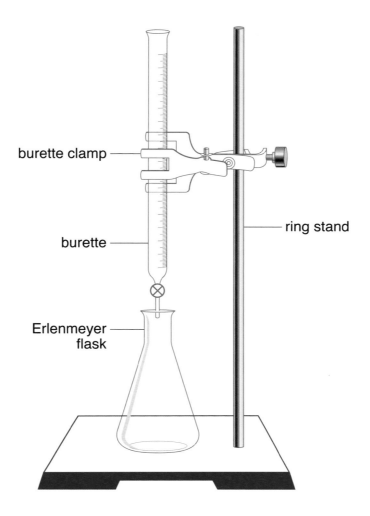

Figure 2

Equipment setup for titration

8. Titrate the solution by adding silver nitrate, one drop at a time, swirling after each addition. Add drops until a red color persists in the flask.

9. When the red color persists, record the final volume of silver nitrate in the burette on the data table. Subtract the two volumes (final – initial) to determine the milliliters of silver nitrate used.

10. Discard the sample, rinse the flask, and repeat the same titration again with another 10 ml of sample 1 so that you have two titrations with the same solution. Record all data on the data table.

11. Repeat steps 4 through 9 with samples 2 and 3.

12. Answer Analysis questions 2 through 7.

Data Table

	Sample 1 Location: _____		Sample 2 Location: _____		Sample 3 Location : _____	
	Trial 1	Trial 2	Trial 1	Trial 2	Trial 1	Trial 2
Initial volume of burette						
Final volume of burette						
Volume of $AgNO_3$ used						
Average volume of $AgNO_3$						
Moles (mol) of $AgNO_3$ used						
Mol of chloride						

Analysis

1. Which sample of water do you think contains the most chloride ions? Explain your reasoning.

2. Find the average volume of $AgNO_3$ used for each sample by adding the volume from both trials and dividing by 2. Record the average on the data table.

3. Use the average volume of $AgNO_3$ for each sample and the compound's *molarity* (0.1 M) to determine the number of moles of $AgNO_3$ used. The formula for molarity is:

$$\text{molarity (M)} = \frac{\text{moles}}{\text{volume (L)}}$$

Record your calculation on the data table.

4. Write the balanced chemical equation for the reaction of chloride ions with silver ions to form silver chloride. What is the mole ratio for silver and chloride?

5. Using the mole ratio of silver to chlorine, determine the mole of chloride contained in each sample.

6. Which water sample contained the most chloride ions? What do you think caused it to have more than the other two?

7. Did your results match your hypothesis in Analysis question 1? If not, explain why it may have been different from what you first thought.

What's Going On?

In a titration, a precise amount of one substance is added to another to react with it. A titration is carried out to its *equivalence point*, the point at which all of the solution in the flask has reacted with the solution from the burette. In this experiment, potassium chromate was used as an indicator to show when the silver nitrate had reacted with all of the chloride ions. Chloride ions react with the silver ions from silver nitrate to form a white *precipitate*. Once all of the chloride ions had reacted with silver, the silver began reacting with the chromate ions from potassium chromate, forming silver chromate, a red precipitate. The lingering red color indicated that all of the chloride ions in the water had been removed.

Because the molarity and the volume of the silver nitrate is known, the moles of silver nitrate involved in the chemical reaction could be determined. Using the balanced chemical reaction for the production of silver chloride from silver ions and chloride ions ($Ag^+ + Cl^- \rightarrow AgCl$), you can determine that one mole of silver is needed to react with each mole of chloride ions. Therefore, the number of moles of chloride in each water sample could be calculated.

Connections

Although it has not been officially documented that trace amounts of chemicals within drinking water can have adverse health effects, many individuals choose to remove these chemicals. There are many filtration techniques that can remove ions from drinking water. Water can be heated to evaporate it then condensed in a purified form in a process called *distillation*. Distillation is effective at disinfecting and removing some chemicals, but it is a slow process and generally filters are more efficient for use in homes.

Two of the most effective and commonly used types of filters in homes are *reverse osmosis* and activated carbon filters. Reverse osmosis filters pressurize water and force it through a *semipermeable membrane* so that only water molecules move through (see Figure 3). These filters can be installed on the main water line to filter all of the water entering a home. In activated carbon filters, water passes through absorbent carbon molecules that react with ions and remove them from the water. Carbon filters are fairly inexpensive and can be used on the main water line entering a house, in the refrigerator, at the tap, or even in specialized filtering pitchers.

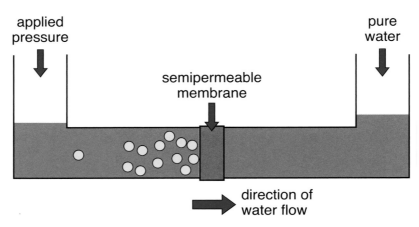

Figure 3

Want to Know More?

See appendix for Our Findings.

Further Reading

American Chemistry Council. "Chlorine Story," 2010. Available online. URL: http://www.americanchemistry.com/s_chlorine/sec_content.asp?CID=1166&DID=4476&CTYPEID=109. Accessed July 17, 2010. This Web site discusses the chemical properties of chlorine.

Clark, Jim. "Test for Halide Ions," 2002. Chemguide. Available online. URL: http://www.chemguide.co.uk/inorganic/group7/testing.html. Accessed July 17, 2010. Clark describes and explains tests for halides (fluoride, chloride, bromide, and iodine) using silver nitrate.

World Health Organization. "Chloride in Drinking-water," March 4, 2003. Originally published in *Guidelines for Drinking-water quality*, 2nd ed. Vol. 2. *Health criteria and other supporting information,* World Health Organization, Geneva, 1996. Available online. URL: http://www.who.int/water_sanitation_health/dwq/chloride.pdf. Accessed July 17, 2010. This article explains the guidelines for safe drinking water, including acceptable levels of chloride compounds.

17. The Rate of Rusting

Topic

The rate at which iron rusts in different solutions can be compared.

Introduction

Have you ever noticed what happens to most metal objects if they are left out in the rain? They tend to rust and corrode. Rust is a reddish-brown substance that often has a flaky or powdery appearance (see Figure 1). Many treatments help to prevent rust formation on metal surfaces. However, once rust forms, it is an irreversible chemical change that can damage the metal substances on which it forms.

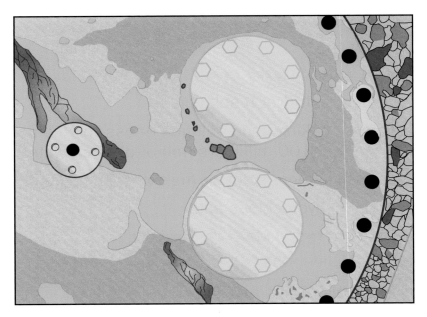

Figure 1

Rust is actually iron oxide

Chemically, rust is iron oxide that forms during the reaction of iron with oxygen. In the process of *oxidation*, iron metal is chemically transformed into iron (II) oxide, FeO. The rate of rust formation is greatly increased by the presence of water. Water penetrates into the tiny pores on the surface of a piece of iron and provides an environment that facilitates the movement of electrons, which increases the rate of the reaction. In this experiment, you will design an experiment to find out how different solutions affect the rate at which rust forms.

Time Required

50 minutes on day 1
10 minutes per day for 5 follow-up days

Materials

- iron wool
- electronic balance
- medium beakers
- graduated cylinder
- tap water
- distilled water
- 15 percent salt (NaCl) solution
- 15 percent baking soda solution (mass-volume percentage: 15 grams [g] per 100 milliliters [ml] of distilled water)
- 50 percent vinegar solution (half vinegar, half distilled water)
- 1 molar (M) hydrochloric acid
- 1 M sodium hydroxide
- forceps
- paper towels
- goggles
- science notebook

Safety Note   Goggles must be worn at all times during this experiment. Use caution when working with acids and bases. Please review and follow the safety guidelines at the beginning of this volume.

Procedure

1. Your job is to design and perform an experiment to determine how the rate at which iron rust forms is affected by four different solutions. Choose any four of these solutions: salt water, baking soda solution, vinegar, hydrochloric acid, and sodium hydroxide.

2. You can use any of the supplies provided by your teacher, but you will not need to use all of them.

3. Before you conduct your experiment, decide exactly what you are going to do. Keep these points in mind:

   a. You must have a way to quantify the amount of rust that forms. For example, you might see if the presence of rust changes the mass of the iron wool, or you could measure how much of the surface of the iron wool changes to rust.

   b. Your experiment needs to have a control group, a sample that is not exposed to any variables.

   c. You will need to check the amount of rust at regualr intervals. Plan to check it once a day for 5 days.

4. Write the steps you plan to take (your experimental procedure) and the materials you plan to use (materials list) on the data table. Show your procedure and materials list to the teacher. If you get teacher approval, proceed with your experiment. If not, modify your work and show it to your teacher again.

5. Once you have teacher approval, assemble the materials you need and begin your procedure.

6. Collect your results on a data table of your own design.

Analysis

1. Write the balanced chemical equation for the formation of rust (iron (II) oxide, FeO) from the reaction of iron (Fe) with oxygen (O_2).

2. Which solutions did you test in your experiment? Why did you choose those solutions?

3. How did you quantify the amount of rust that formed on the iron?

4. Rank the samples that you tested in order of their ability to increase the rate of rusting. (1 = least rust, 4 = most)

5. Which sample(s) of iron corroded the most? The least?

6. Why do you think some solutions caused more rusting than others?

Data Table	
Your procedure	
Your materials list	
Teacher's approval	

What's Going On?

In the process of rusting, iron metal (Fe_{metal}) loses electrons at one location, known as the *anode*, and gains them at another, the *cathode*. This causes oxygen, which is at the cathode, to gain electrons and become hydroxide (OH^-). The hydroxide joins with the positively charged iron atoms to form an intermediate compound, iron (II) hydroxide, $Fe(OH)_2$, near the anode area. The $Fe(OH)_2$ is then even further oxidized by the oxygen dissolved in the water to form Fe^{+3} and water. Excess oxygen in the water or in the atmosphere is attracted to the iron ions at the anode area because of their positive charge. When excess oxygen joins with the Fe^{+3}, it forms rust, iron (III) oxide (see Figure 2).

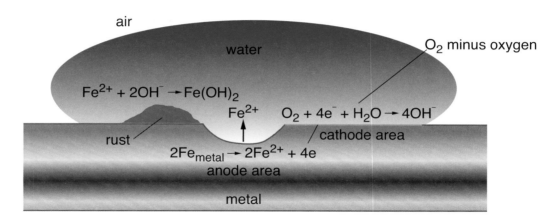

Figure 2

Formation of rust on iron

Such *oxidation-reduction (redox)* reactions occur much more easily when electrons flow freely. The movement of electrons is greatly increased in *electrolyte* solutions, or solutions that contain charged particles. Therefore, if a salt is dissolved in water it will increase the rate of rusting. This is why objects generally rust faster in salt water than in freshwater. Acids and bases tend to increase the rate of rusting even more than salt because they are much stronger electrolytes. Because acids and bases are corrosive, they will often dissolve the rust that is produced, and it may not observed; however, if the mass of the substance is measured, one will see that the object has undergone corrosion even though rust does not appear on the surface.

Connections

Water is a *polar* molecule. The oxygen atom in a water molecule attracts the shared electrons, giving it a slight negative charge. The two hydrogen atoms of water have a slight positive charge because the electrons are pulled away from them (see Figure 3). As a polar molecule, water has the ability to dissolve many substances, creating charged particles called *ions*. Water naturally contains a relatively high concentration of a variety of ions. Most of these ions are not harmful and actually give drinking water a more pleasant taste. However, other ions found in water are not very desirable. Sulfate ions tend to give water an unpleasant smell and taste. Iron and manganese ions discolor water and affect its taste as well. Calcium ions can cause buildup on pipes and in sinks and bathtubs and cause soap not to lather as easily. Because many ions are undesirable, many people choose to have special filters installed into their homes or sinks to remove these ions from their drinking water.

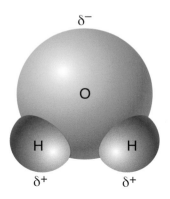

Figure 3

A water molecule has a slight negative charge near the oxygen atom and slight positive charges near the hydrogen atoms.

Want to Know More?

See appendix for Our Findings.

Further Reading

Chemistry Daily. "Rust," 2005. Available online. URL: http://www. chemistrydaily.com/chemistry/Rust. Accessed July 17, 2010. This Web site explains the movement of electrons in oxidation of iron.

Hendlin, Lily, Trevor Lieberman, and Karli Cowman. "Dissolved Ions in Natural Fresh Water." Available online. URL:http://drake.marin.k12.ca.us/ stuwork/ROCKwater/Dissolved%20Ions/an%20introduction%20to%20 dissolved%20ions.html. Accessed July 17, 2010. The authors explain how ions make their way into bodies of fresh water in this article.

Ophardt, Charles D. Virtual ChemBook. "Formation of Ionic Iron Oxide" 2003. Available online. URL: http://www.elmhurst.edu/~chm/ vchembook/143Afeoxide.html. Accessed July 17, 2010. The Web site examines the roles of the valence electrons of iron and oxygen in the formation of iron rust.

18. Thin Layer Chromatography

Topic

Over-the-counter analgesics can be characterized using thin layer chromatography.

Introduction

Pain relievers, or *analgesics*, come in many different varieties. Pharmaceutical companies spend millions of dollars each year on advertisements claiming that their brands of pain relievers are the best and most effective. Most types of analgesics contain different combinations of just a few common compounds. Some of the most widely used compounds in pain relievers include aspirin, acetaminophen, and ibuprofen. These compounds, some of which are shown in Figure 1, are often combined with caffeine, a mild stimulant that counteracts the sedative effects of the pain reliever.

In the laboratory, the components of an over-the-counter pain reliever can be determined using *thin layer chromatography* (TLC), a technique that separates compounds based on their size or polarity. Compounds are placed in small spots on a plate coated with a substance such as silica or alumina gel. The plate is placed in a container with *solvent* that dissolves the spotted solution and carries it up the chromatography plate as it moves upward. Different components of the solution will "fall out" of solution as the solvent moves up the plate. The distance that the substance travels varies based on the chemical composition of that substance. For this reason, TLC can be used to identify the components of an over-the-counter analgesic tablet if compared to known solutions. In this experiment, you will perform thin layer chromatography on four known solutions and two unknown solutions made from over-the-counter analgesic tablets. You will then compare the results and determine which compounds are present in the unknown tablets.

Figure 1

**Aspirin, acetaminophen, and ibuprofen are some
over-the-counter analgesics.**

Time Required

60 minutes

Materials

- ◦ 5 silica-coated chromatography plates (precut)
- ◦ microcapillary tubes
- ◦ 5 developing chambers (small jars with lids)
- ◦ standard chromatography solutions (premixed) for:
  - ✔ aspirin
  - ✔ acetaminophen
  - ✔ caffeine
  - ✔ ibuprofen
- ◦ several over-the-counter analgesic tablets of various brands such as Excedrin™, Aspirin™, Midol™, Tylenol™, Advil™, and Anacin™.
- ◦ knife
- ◦ mortar and pestle
- ◦ spatula
- ◦ small test tubes
- ◦ test-tube rack
- ◦ 95 percent ethanol
- ◦ ethyl acetate/acetic acid solvent (95 percent ethyl acetate; 5 percent glacial acetic acid)
- ◦ Pasteur pipette
- ◦ tweezers

- pencil
- ruler
- UV lamp
- calculator
- goggles
- science notebook

Procedure

1. Prepare the five silica-coated thin layer chromatography plates. To do so:

    a. Using a ruler, measure 1 centimeter (cm) from the bottom of each plate and draw a straight line across the plate in pencil, as shown in Figure 2. Draw the lines on the white surface of the plate and be careful not to scratch the surface.

    b. Label the bottom of each plate under the line, in pencil, with the analgesic used: "aspirin," "acetaminophen," "caffeine," "ibuprofen," or "unknown."

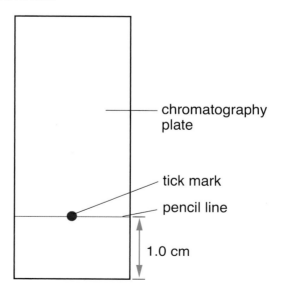

Figure 2

TLC plate preparation

2. Spot each of the four known (aspirin, acetaminophen, caffeine, and ibuprofen) plates with their appropriate solutions. To do so:

   a. Draw a faint tick mark in pencil in the center of the line that was drawn across the bottom of the plate.

   b. Dip a microcapillary tube into the solution so that some of the solution is taken up.

   c. Place the tip of the tube onto the chromatography plate on top of the tick mark, leaving a spot of solution.

   d. Allow the spot to dry.

   e. Repeat four times with the same solution on the same spot.

   f. Repeat steps a through e with the three remaining standard solutions, using clean microcapillary tubes with each sample.

3. Choose one of the analgesic tablets provided by your instructor. Record the name of the analgesic on Data Table 1. (Analgesics may include Excedrin™, Midol™, Tylenol™, Advil™, and Anacin™.)

4. Prepare a solution of one of the analgesic tablets. To do so:

   a. Carefully cut the tablet into fourths using a knife. You will only need one-quarter of the tablet. Return the remaining portion to your instructor to be used by other students.

   b. Crush the one-quarter tablet into a powder using a mortar and pestle.

   c. Label a small test tube with the name of the analgesic/unknown you are using. Scrape the crushed tablet into the test tube.

   d. Add approximately 1 milliliter (ml) of 95 percent ethanol into the test tube and shake vigorously for 45 seconds (sec) to 1 minute (min). Set the test tube aside and allow solid particles to settle.

   e. Repeat steps a through d with the second analgesic tablet.

5. Spot the two analgesic solutions on a TLC plate. To do so:

   a. Draw two tick marks on the line across the bottom of the unknown TLC plate. The marks should be evenly spaced so that the solutions will not overlap and will not run into the edge of the plate.

   b. Place a clean microcapillary tube into the test tube containing analgesic sample 1 so that some of the solution is taken up.

    c. Place the tip of the tube on the first tick mark. Allow the solution to dry and repeat four more times on the same spot with the same solution.

    d. Repeat the process with the second sample, using a new microcapillary tube and placing the spot on the second tic mark.

6. Pour about 0.5 cm of ethyl acetate/acetic acid solvent into the bottom of five developing chambers.

7. Place each TLC plate into a container of solvent with the pencil line side down (see Figure 3). The solvent should not reach the pencil line. Tighten the lid on each jar.

8. Allow the solvent to travel up the plate. Remove the plate, using tweezers, when the solvent is about 1 cm from the top of the plate.

9. Mark the "solvent front" on each plate using a pencil. This is the point where the solvent stopped.

10. Dispose of the solutions used in the specified organic waste container.

11. View the plates under a UV lamp to see how far each solution traveled. Notice that the standard solutions contain only one ingredient, so they have one spot that moved up the plate with the solvent. The analgesics are mixtures, and each of their components created a spot.

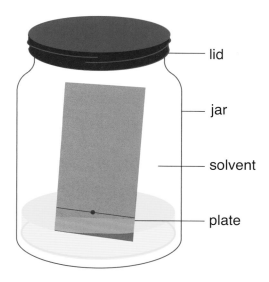

Figure 3

TLC plate in developing chamber

Data Table			
Solution	Distance solvent moved	Distance solution moved	R_f value
Aspirin			
Acetaminophen			
Caffeine			
Ibuprofen			
Unknown 1 _____		1.	
		2.	
		3.	
		4.	
Unknown 2 _____		1.	
		2.	
		3.	
		4.	

Analysis

1. For each of the TLC plates, measure the distance from the bottom pencil line, or origin, to the solvent front (top line) in centimeters. The two unknown solutions will have the same measurements, because they were on the same plate. Record these values on the data table.

2. For each of the standard solutions, measure the distance from the origin to the center of the sample spot. Record these values on the data table under "Distance solution moved."

3. For the unknown samples, measure the distance that each component traveled (from the origin to the center of the spot). Record these measurements on the data table.

4. Calculate the R_f value for each of the solutions and the components using the data recorded on the data table.

$$R_f = \frac{\text{distance solution traveled}}{\text{distance solvent traveled}}$$

5. Compare the R_f values for the two unknown solutions with those for the four known TLC plates. Which components do you think each of your unknown samples contains?

6. Did any spots appear on the unknown sample plates that did not match a known solution? What do you think those components might be?

7. Why was it important to draw your origin line in pencil and not pen?

8. How might your results be different if you used too much of each solution? If you did not use enough?

What's Going On?

Thin layer chromatography requires a solvent that will attract the solutions on the baseline strongly enough to move them up the plate, but not so much that they form strong bonds with the compound. As the solvent rises, the force of gravity pulls the compound and solvent apart. The solvent used in this lab was a 95:5 mixture of ethyl acetate and acetic acid. Because it has slightly *polar* and nonpolar characteristics, it can attract the components in the analgesics long enough to move them away from the baseline, but not all the way to the solvent front. The components of the known solutions behave the same way as those identical components present in the analgesic tablets because they have the same chemical structure. The porous silica coating on the TLC plate locks each compound in place until it can be viewed. Compounds on a silica plate are often difficult to see without the use of a UV light or a stain such as iodine.

Connections

Thin layer chromatography is just one type of chromatography that is used to separate compounds. Paper chromatography can separate dyes and colored compounds from solutions. This type of chromatography uses a porous type of paper, such as filter paper, and a nonpolar or slightly polar solvent to carry the compounds up the paper. Paper chromatography will separate the different components of ink and dyes to determine which compounds were used to make the solution that color. For instance, a black marker that is deemed to be "permanent" because it does not dissolve in water, may separate into red, blue, yellow, and green components when it is dissolved in a polar solvent. Paper chromatography can also be used to separate photosynthetic *pigments* in plants. Most green plants appear green because they have a dominant green pigment, which is usually *chlorophyll A*, but they will often contain many accessory pigments such as *xanthophyll* and *carotenoids* to absorb various wavelengths of light. Much like thin layer chromatography, the pigments separated by paper chromatography travel up the paper based on the size of the molecule and its solubility in the solvent that is used.

Want to Know More?

See appendix for Our Findings.

Further Reading

Clark, Jim. "Thin Layer Chromatography," 2007. Chemguide. Available online. URL: http://www.chemguide.co.uk/analysis/chromatography/thinlayer.html. Accessed July 17, 2010. Clark explains how to carry out thin layer chromatography and discusses some of the uses of this technique.

"Thin Layer Chromatography," July 13, 2008. Available online. URL: http://www.youtube.com/watch?v=_TqGAnK9Rkw. Accessed July 17, 2010. In this YouTube video, a students carries out thin layer chromatography and explains the technique.

"Thin Layer Chromatography–TLC." CU Boulder Organic Chemistry Undergrad Courses, Lab Techniques. Available online. URL: http://orgchem.colorado.edu/hndbksupport/TLC/TLC.html. Accessed July 17, 2010. This Web site troubleshoots some of the problems one may encountered when using TLC in the lab.

19. Levels of Sugar

Topic

The sugar concentration of a commercial fruit juice can be determined by comparing its density to densities of calibrated sugar solutions.

Introduction

People who are watching their caloric intake may be accustomed to reading the labels on food items, but some are not aware of the *calories* found in beverages. Generally, fruit juices are promoted as healthy choices and good alternatives to sodas. However, most fruit juices have just as much, or even more, sugar in them than sodas and soft drinks. Fruits are naturally high in simple sugars, *fructose* and *glucose*. Therefore, even if fruit juice beverages claim to have "no sugar added," they still have very high sugar content. Additionally, many producers of fruit juice add more *sucrose* to enhance the flavor and drinkability. Sucrose, or table sugar, is made of a molecule of glucose bonded to a molecule of fructose, as shown in Figure 1.

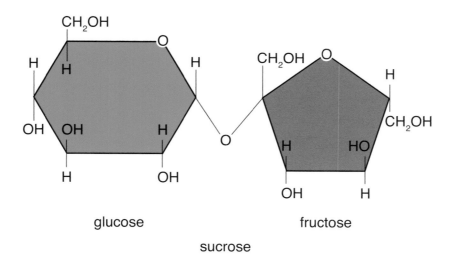

Figure 1

Sucrose is a disaccharide made of one glucose molecule and one fructose molecule.

Sugar is a very dense molecule, making up the majority of the mass and density of most fruit juices and sugary beverages. The sugar concentration of drinks can be determined based on the *density* of the liquid in comparison to sugar solutions of known sucrose concentration. In this experiment, you will measure the density of sucrose solutions of known concentration and create a calibration curve. You will then measure the density of several fruit juices and compare them to the values on the calibration curve in order to determine their sugar content.

Time Required

30 minutes

Materials

- ●◇ electronic balance
- ●◇ graduated cylinder (10 to 25 milliliters [ml])
- ●◇ small cups or beakers (25 to 50 ml, 10 per laboratory group)
- ●◇ calculator
- ●◇ standard sucrose solutions (percent mass/volume): 0 percent, 5 percent, 10 percent, 15 percent, 20 percent, and 25 percent
- ●◇ various commercial fruit juices (such as apple, grape, cherry, orange, and mixed fruit)
- ●◇ spray cleaner
- ●◇ paper towels
- ●◇ graph paper
- ●◇ ruler
- ●◇ science notebook

Safety Note   **Please review and follow the safety guidelines at the beginning of this volume.**

Procedure

1. Obtain the five standard sucrose solutions and place them into small cups or beakers labeled as 0 percent, 5 percent, 10 percent, 15 percent, 20 percent, and 25 percent.

2. Place a cup or beaker onto the electronic balance and tare the balance.

3. Measure 10 ml of the first standard solution into a graduated cylinder. Pour the solution into the cup on the balance and record its mass on Data Table 1.

4. Pour the contents of the cup on the balance back into the labeled cup or beaker, rinse and dry the "measuring" cup.

5. Repeat steps 2 thorugh 4 for each of the standard solutions.

6. Choose four different fruit juices and place them in small, labeled cups or beakers. Which one do you think will have the most sugar? The least? Write these predictions in your science notebook.

7. Place the cup or beaker for measuring mass back onto the balance and zero it.

8. Measure 10 ml of the first juice into a graduated cylinder. Pour it into the cup on the balance and record its mass on Data Table 2.

9. Empty the cup on the balance back into your labeled cup or beaker, rinse and dry the "measuring" cup.

10. Repeat steps 7 through 9 for each of the fruit juice samples.

11. Return the standard solutions to the containers indicated by your teacher to be reused, or pour them down the sink if instructed to do so.

Data Table 1			
Percent m/v of sucrose	Mass (g)	Volume (ml)	Density (g/ml)
0		10	
5		10	
10		10	
15		10	
20		10	
25		10	

Data Table 2				
Fruit juice	Mass (g)	Volume (ml)	Density (g/ml)	Percent sucrose (concentration)
1.		10		
2.		10		
3.		10		
4.		10		

Analysis

1. Calculate the density for each of the standard solutions on Data Table 1 using the formula

    $$D = \frac{m}{v}$$

    where D is density, m is mass, and v is volume. Record these values on Data Table 1.

2. Graph the percent sucrose versus the density of the standard solutions on a piece of graph paper. Place concentration (percent sucrose) on the X-axis and the density on the Y-axis. Be sure to label all axes and use proper scaling for all measurements. Connect the plots to create a calibration curve similar to the one in Figure 2.

3. Calculate the density for each of the fruit juices that you recorded on Data Table 2 using the formula same formula:

    $$D = \frac{m}{v}$$

    Record the densities on Data Table 2.

4. Plot the density of the first fruit juice you measured on the calibration curve you created in step 2 and find where the point plotted on the curve meets the concentration (percentage m/v of sucrose). Record the concentration in Data Table 2. Repeat for each of the fruit juice samples.

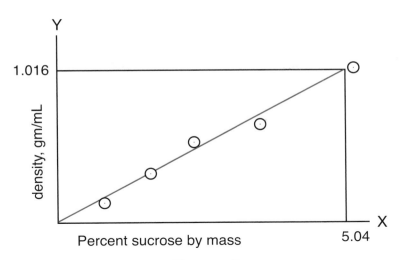

Figure 2

Sample calibration curve

5. Rank the juices you measured from 1 to 4, with 1 having the lowest sugar concentration and 4 having the highest.

6. Did your findings agree with your predictions? Why or why not?

7. Read the labels of the fruit juice containers and determine the grams of sugar per serving for the juices that you tested. Does this correlate to your findings? Why or why not?

What's Going On?

Sucrose is a fairly heavy *disaccharide* molecule, composed of one glucose and one fructose molecule. Glucose and fructose are typically found naturally in fruits and fruit juices; since these molecules make up sucrose, the densities of all three types of sugar are extremely similar. Therefore, a standardized solution of sucrose can accurately assess the density of sugar found in fruit juices. Because fruit juices are predominantly made up of water and sugar, the density of the solution is correlated to the amount of sugar contained in the solution. A calibration curve created by plotting the densities of known solutions compared to their concentration can be used to determine the concentration of the unknown fruit juices based on where they fall on the curve. The results of this experiment show that fruit juices contain as much as sodas, or even more. Figure 3 illustrates this point, making it clear that sodas such as Sprite™, Pepsi™, and Coca-Cola™ Classic average about 27 grams of sugar per serving. On the other hand, fruit drinks have more sugar, and therefore more calories. Grape juice is the worst offender with 36 grams of sugar per serving.

Beverage	Calories		Total sugar (g)	
Sprite™	■■■■■■	100	■■	26
Pepsi™	■■■■■■	100	■■	28
Coca-Cola™ Classic	■■■■■■	97	■■	27
Gatorade G Cool Blue™	■■■	50	■	14
grape Juice	■■■■■■■■■	152	■■	36
pineapple juice	■■■■■■■■	132	■■	25
cranberry juice	■■■■■■■	116	■■	31
apple juice	■■■■■■■	114	■■	24
orange juice	■■■■■■■	112	■■	21
grapefruit juice	■■■■■	96	■■	22

Sources: U.S. Department of Agriculture Nutrient Data Laboratory; company information graphics reporting by Karen Kaplan.

Figure 3

Calorie and sugar content of selected beverages
per 8-ounce (oz) (.24 liters [L]) serving: all juices are unsweetened

Connections

In some industries, it is very important to be able to determine accurately the concentration of sugar in solutions. Examples of these industries include those that produce syrups, candies, sorbets, ice cream, and alcoholic beverages. In order to have high-quality finished products, makers must know the composition of the starting material. For instance, if a candymaker uses too much sugar while making caramel, the sugars will crystallize and give the candy a crunchy texture, which is not desirable in caramel. If the sugar concentration in ice cream or sorbet is too high, the product may not freeze properly and may not have the desirable creamy texture. If the sugar concentration in syrup is too low, it will be thin and watery; if it is too high, it will be cloudy and may crystallize. In the production of alcoholic beverages, a high sugar content yields a higher alcohol content in the finished product. Therefore, it is very important to be able to determine accurately the concentration of sugar in solutions before a process has begun.

There are two common ways of determining the concentration of sugar in solutions. The first method involves measuring the density, or *specific gravity*, of the solution. This measurement requires a device known as a *saccharometer*, a type of *hydrometer* that uses the *buoyancy* of the device placed in a solution to measure its density. The second method for determining the concentration of sugar in a solution is by the *refraction* of light in a solution. This technique requires a *refractometer*, a device that measures how much light is bent, or refracted within a solution. The degree of refraction can be correlated to concentration of solutes within that solution. Some refractometers are available as handheld devices with a digital output for quick and easy data collection.

Want to Know More?

See appendix for Our Findings.

Further Reading

Hall, Dave. "Hooked on Juice," October 2, 2006. Available online. URL: http://www.hookedonjuice.com/. Accessed July 17, 2010. Hall is a newspaper editor with an interest in nutrition. This Web page compare the sugar content of fruit juices to other beverages.

Nave, Robert. "Glucose." HyperPhysics. Available online. URL: http://hyperphysics.phy-astr.gsu.edu/hbase/Organic/sugar.html. Accessed July 17, 2010. On this Web page, hosted by Georgia State University, the author discusses the chemical structures of simple sugars and other carbohydrates.

Ophardt, Charles D. "Sucrose," 2003. Virtual ChemBook. Available online. URL: http://www.elmhurst.edu/~chm/vchembook/546sucrose.html. Accessed July 17, 2010. On this Web page, Ophardt explains how sucrose molecules form from glucose and fructose units.

20. Microscale Percent Composition

Topic

The percent composition of carbon dioxide in a carbonated beverage can be determined using a sample of the gas extracted with a syringe.

Introduction

The British physician Joseph Priestley (1733–1804) created the first carbonated beverage, soda water. Priestly enjoyed the bubbly water as a beverage, but other scientists felt that the fizzy quality of the water gave it health benefits. Many pharmacists made and sold soda water, also known as soft drinks, over the counter. The development of a bottling technique made it possible for customers to take their "remedies" home. These early carbonated beverages sold in pharmacies were either natural mineral water or water infused that carbon dioxide that contained vitamins and herbal flavorings. The drinks eventually became more popular for their taste than for their health benefits.

The "fizz," or carbonation, in soda is due to dissolved carbon dioxide gas. When a gas is added to a liquid under high pressure and low temperature, the gas dissolves into the solution. If the pressure is released, the gas comes out of solution, making the hissing sound associated with opening a soda. Carbon dioxide that is not lost during opening is slowly released as bubbles, which causes the fizz in sodas and sparkling water. In this experiment, you will use a syringe like the one shown in Figure 1 to extract carbon dioxide from a carbonated beverage and determine the percent composition of carbon dioxide dissolved in the solution.

Time Required

30 minutes

Materials

- microscale gas syringe
- syringe cap

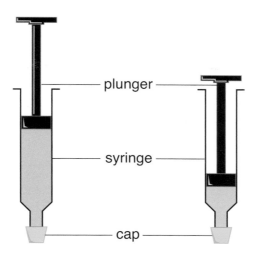

Figure 1

Microscale gas syringe

- ice-cold sparkling water or sugar-free carbonated drink
- electronic balance
- calculator
- goggles
- science notebook

Safety Note Goggles must be worn at all times during this experiment. Work carefully with liquids under pressure, which may cause unintended spraying. Please review and follow the safety guidelines at the beginning of this volume.

Procedure

1. Use the electronic balance to find the mass of a microscale gas syringe with a cap in grams (g). Record this mass on the data table.

2. Remove the plunger from the syringe, be sure that the cap is in place, invert the syringe, and slowly pour about 15 to 20 milliliters (ml) of the cold carbonated drink into the syringe. Try to avoid releasing gas bubbles as you pour.

3. Replace the plunger into the end of the syringe so that the rubber stopper is just inside of the bottom rim.

4. Slowly turn the syringe so that the tip is facing upward and carefully remove the cap.

5. Press the plunger upward to release all of the air from above the solution, so that the liquid fills the tip of the syringe. Replace the syringe cap.

6. Find the mass of the syringe filled with carbonated drink. Record the mass on the data table. Allow the solution in the syringe to reach room temperature. (You can warm the beverage with your hands to speed the process if desired.)

7. Pull the syringe plunger back, creating a negative pressure that will pull carbon dioxide gas out of the solution. Tap the side of the syringe until bubbles are no longer being formed. Pull the syringe plunger back as far as you can without removing it from the device, then release it so that it will return to equilibrium. Tap the syringe again, then pull the plunger back and release it once more.

8. Be sure that the tip of the syringe is facing upward and remove the cap. Push the plunger in to expel all of the carbon dioxide, but none of the liquid, from the syringe. Replace the cap.

9. Find the mass of the syringe and solution and record your findings on the data table.

10. Remove the cap and plunger from the syringe. Pour the liquid down the sink and rinse out the syringe.

Data Table	
Measurement	**Mass (g)**
Syringe (including cap)	
Syringe and carbonated drink	
Syringe and drink with CO_2 removed	
Mass of Carbonated drink (syringe with beverage − mass of syringe)	
Mass of drink without CO_2 (syringe and beverage with CO_2 removed − mass of syringe)	
Mass of CO_2 (syringe with carbonated drink − syringe with CO_2 removed)	

Analysis

1. Find the mass of the carbonated drink by subtracting the mass of the syringe from the mass of the syringe and beverage together. Record this value on the data table.

2. Subtract the mass of the syringe from the mass of the syringe with the drink after the carbon dioxide was removed to find the mass of the beverage without carbon dioxide. Record this value on the data table as the mass of the beverage in the syringe.

3. Find the mass of the carbon dioxide in the drink by subtracting the mass of the drink with carbon dioxide removed from the mass of the syringe with carbonated drink in it. Record this value on the data table.

4. For the purposes of this lab, assume that the beverage being tested is pure water, H_2O. Using the mass of the water to represent the drink with carbon dioxide removed (from the data table) and the molar (M) mass for water, calculate the number of moles of water in the sample.

5. Use the mass of carbon dioxide from the data table and the molar mass of CO_2 to determine the number of moles of CO_2 collected.

6. Determine the ratio of moles of water to moles of carbon dioxide found in the drink:

    $$\frac{\text{mol } H_2O}{\text{mol } CO_2}$$

7. Multiply the ratio from Analysis question 6 by the M mass of water. Add this number to the M mass of carbon dioxide. This is the M mass of the carbonated drink that you tested.

8. Find the percent composition of carbon dioxide in the drink by dividing the M mass of carbon dioxide by the M mass of the carbonated drink and multiplying by 100 to obtain a percentage.

9. Why did the carbon dioxide leave the drink when you pulled the syringe back?

10. Why was it important for the drink to be cold when you poured it into the syringe? Why was it warmed before extracting the CO_2?

What's Going On?

The particles of matter in a gas behave differently from those in a liquid. In a gas, particles are spread out and move at relatively high speeds;

in a liquid, the particles are much closer together and their movement is slower. Gases, such as carbon dioxide, can be dissolved into liquid solutions, but to do so requires that the molecules of the gas to be compressed and slowed down. Compression is done by increasing the pressure of the liquid and gas so that they can form a mixture. Figure 2 shows how increasing pressure helps mix the molecules of a gas and liquid. When the pressure is decreased, dissolved gases separate from the mixture and become vaporous again. This is the case with carbonated beverages, which contain carbon dioxide dissolved into liquids to give a distinctive taste and texture. Carbonated drinks such as mineral water or sodas must be sealed in a container such as a can or bottle to keep the carbon dioxide in solution. If the drink is heated or left open for an extended amount of time, the carbon dioxide separates from the solution and the drink goes "flat."

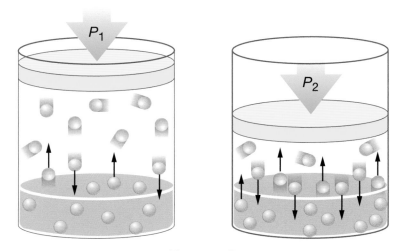

Figure 2

**Increasing pressure from P_1 to P_2 forces more
gas molecules to dissolve in a liquid.**

The *percent composition* of a substance is the amount of that particular substance compared to the amount of the entire compound. In chemistry, amounts are measured in moles. Therefore, to find the percent composition of carbon dioxide in carbonated water, you must first know how many molecules of carbon dioxide there are in solution compared to the number of water molecules. This is done by turning the mass of each substance into moles to find the ratio of water to carbon dioxide. The ratio of molecules is used to determine the chemical composition of the solution. Once the chemical composition of the solution is known, the percent composition of carbon dioxide in the solution can be calculated by dividing the mass of carbon dioxide by the mass of the entire solution and multiplying by 100 percent.

Connections

Organisms that live in the water, such as fish and aquatic invertebrates, depend on oxygen gas dissolved in water. Animals and many other organisms require oxygen for *cellular respiration*, a biochemical process that converts the energy in glucose to adenosine triphosphate (ATP). Oxygen enters waterways through *photosynthesis* or *aeration*. Generally, plants and algae within aquatic ecosystems produce enough oxygen through photosynthesis to maintain high concentrations of the gas. Fast-moving waterways also incorporate oxygen when the water flows over rocks and other rough surfaces, mixing atmospheric oxygen with the water.

Pollution is one of the primary causes of low oxygen in waterways. When pollutants run into rivers, streams, and lakes, the amount of dissolved oxygen is decreased in a process known as *eutrophication*. The worst pollutants are those that carry high levels of nutrients, such as agricultural runoff, sewage, animal waste, and industrial wastes. The excess nutrients support the growth of algae. When the algae die, they are consumed by fast-growing populations of bacteria that use up the oxygen in the water. Loss of oxygen due to eutrophication can lead to massive death of fish and other aquatic animals that need the dissolved oxygen to survive.

Want to Know More?

See appendix for Our Findings.

Further Reading

Aus-e-tute. "Percent Composition." Available online. URL: http://www. ausetute.com.au/percentc.html. Accessed July 17, 2010. This Web site explains how to find percent compositions and provides sample calculations.

Bellis, Mary. "Introduction to Pop: The History of Soft Drinks," 2010. About.com. Available online. URL: http://inventors.about.com/od/ foodrelatedinventions/a/soft_drinks.htm. Accessed July 17, 2010. Bellis explains the formulas and marketing of early carbonated beverages in this article.

The Human Touch of Chemistry: Famous Scientists. "Joseph Priestley." Available online. URL: http://www.humantouchofchemistry.com/node/39. Accessed July 17, 2010. This brief biography describes Priestley's scientific work including research into oxygen gas and the mechanism of photosynthesis.

Scope and Sequence Chart

This chart aligns the experiments in this book with some of the National Science Content Standards. (These experiments do not address every national science standard.) Please refer to your local and state content standards for additional information. As always, adult supervision is recommended and discretion should be used in selecting experiments appropriate to each age group or to individual students.

Standard	Grades 5–8	Grades 9–12
Physical Science		
Properties and changes of properties in matter	all	all
Chemical reactions	all	all
Motions and forces		
Transfer of energy and interactions of energy and matter	9, 12, 15	9, 12, 15
Conservation of energy and increase in disorder		
Life Science		
Cells and structure and function in living systems		
Reproduction and heredity		
Regulation and behavior		

Standard	Grades 5–8	Grades 9–12
Populations and ecosystems		
Diversity and adaptations of organisms		
Interdependence of organisms		
Matter, energy, and organization in living systems		
Biological evolution		
Earth Science		
Structure and energy in the Earth system		
Geochemical cycles		
Origin and evolution of the Earth system		
Origin and evolution of the universe		
Earth in the solar system		
Nature of Science		
Science in history	20	20
Science as an endeavor	all	all

Grade Level

Title of Experiment	Grade Level
1. The Smell of an Ester	6–12
2. The Chemistry of Toothpaste	6–12
3. Water Softeners	6–12
4. Lewis Structures	6–12
5. Making Soap	6–12
6. Ozone Depletion	6–12
7. Catalysis of Hydrogen Peroxide	6–12
8. Wood Alcohol	9–12
9. Solutes Affect the Boiling Point of Water	6–12
10. Potable Water	6–12
11. Solutions and Spectrophotometry	9–12
12. Endothermic and Exothermic Reactions	6–12
13. Finding Molar Mass	9–12
14. Chemical Moles	9–12
15. Heat Energy	6–12
16. Chloride Levels	6–12
17. The Rate of Rusting	6–12
18. Thin Layer Chromatography	6–12
19. Levels of Sugar	6–12
20. Microscale Percent Composition	6–12

Setting

All the experiments involve materials and equipment found only in science laboratories and must be carried out there. Always wear goggles and close–toed shoes when working in the chemistry lab. Students should pay close attention to the specific safety notes in the experiments because some chemicals and laboratory equipment can be quite hazardous. The work of one lab group can potentially endanger students nearby if safety is not a priority. Review the location of all safety equipment. All experiments require adult supervision.

Our Findings

Idea for class discussion: Ask students to name some of their favorite scents or flavors in foods and perfumes. Discuss the fact that often manufacturers do not use natural flavors and scents in their products.

Analysis

1. Answers will vary depending on the esters selected by students.

Ester Name	Structure
Methyl butyrate	
Methyl benzoate	
Methyl cinnamate	
Ethyl cinnamate	
Ethyl formate	
Ethyl salicylate	
Ethyl heptanoate	

Isobutyl formate	
Butyl butyrate	
Pentyl acetate	
Pentyl butyrate	
Octyl acetate	

2. Answers will vary based on student observations. The scent of alcohols and acids are generally very volatile and potent, while esters tend to be much more pleasant.

3. Answers will vary based on student results and observations. Reasons for the scent differing from the expected odor may be human error, scent perception differences among individuals, or failure to allow the chemicals to react completely.

4. If the test tubes were not heated or sulfuric acid were not added, there would be equal amounts of product and reactant and the scent of the ester product would not be evident.

5. Answers will vary. Esters are commonly produced to be used as artificial flavorings for food and candy as well as scents for candles, potpourri, and scented oils.

2. THE CHEMISTRY OF TOOTHPASTE

Idea for class discussion: Ask a few students to name their favorite brands or types of toothpaste. Find out what they prefer about these favorites.

Analysis

1. Answers will vary based on toothpastes chosen. Whitening toothpastes may contain hydrogen peroxide or sodium carbonate peroxide; tartar control toothpastes may contain tetrasodium

pyrophosphate; toothpastes for sensitive teeth may contain potassium citrate, potassium nitrate, or strontium chloride. Some toothpastes may contain variations of the surfactants (lauryl sulfates) or antibacterial agents (usually triclosan, glycerin, or zinc).

2. Answers will vary based on individual student predictions. Students should choose the sample they feel will be the most acidic/basic, have the most fluoride, be the most abrasive, create the most foam, etc.

3. Answers will vary based on experimental results. Students should explain whether or not the results matched their predictions and why they feel that they got the results that they did.

4. Answers will vary based on student results and the toothpaste samples chosen. For example, toothpastes with higher amounts of baking soda, surfactants, and antimicrobial substances will have a higher pH. Toothpastes with whitening agents are generally more acidic. Those with a higher amount of sodium lauryl sulfate will produce more foam; and those with more hydrated silica, silicon dioxide, or titanium dioxide will be more abrasive.

5. Answers will vary based on toothpastes chosen. Students should compare different brands of toothpaste that claim to be of the same variety and describe the differences in ingredients and properties based on brand name alone.

6. Answers will vary based on student results. Students should describe how the differences in properties were based on the ingredients in each of the samples tested.

3. WATER SOFTENERS

Idea for class discussion: Ask students if they have ever seen dark–colored deposits of minerals in sinks, tubs, or toilets. Explain that some dark rings are due to minerals in the water. Have students explain how minerals get into water, and why the mineral content of different bodies of water will vary.

Analysis

1. Answers will vary depending on the methods chosen. Students should describe their procedure in distillation or ion replacement using lime and soda ash or ion replacement resin and describe their reasons for choosing the two methods that they did.

2. Answers will vary based on student procedures. Students should describe the control factors that they used, such as the volume of water, amount of ion replacement materials used, etc. Control factors are important in science experiments to ensure that the factor that is being tested is only affected by one variable.

3. Hard water contains ions such as calcium and magnesium that can combine with soap to create an insoluble film that hinders the foaming ability of soap and can create "soap scum" stains. Softened water only contains sodium ions, which are the same ions present in soap, so they do not hinder the foaming ability of soap.

4. Naturally occurring minerals in groundwater cause water to become hard. The minerals that become dissolved in water differ depending on the geology of the area.

5. Hard water tends to be the most common in the Midwest and central United States. The areas with higher concentrations of ions in groundwater usually have more arid climates and sandy or very mineralized soil.

6. Many water softeners add sodium to the water, which is a health concern for individuals with high blood pressure or heart problems. It can also cause the water to taste salty. Softened water contains excessive amounts of sodium ions that can cause soap to cling to the skin and make it harder to wash soap off in order to have a "clean" feeling.

4. LEWIS STRUCTURES

Idea for class discussion: Ask students to explain the location of electrons in atoms. Discuss the number and arrangement of orbitals in two or three types of atoms.

Note to the teacher: Covalent compounds are N_2, CH_4, NH_3, CO_2, H_2, PCl_3, H_2O. Ionic compounds are LiBr, $CaCl_2$, KI, Na_2O, SrF_2.

Analysis

1. Answers may vary. Students should include three comparisons, which may include the following: Atoms share electrons in covalent bonds, but electrons are exchanged in ionic bonds. Covalent bonds occur between nonmetals and ionic bonds occur between a metal and nonmetal. Covalent bonds are much stronger than ionic bonds. Ionic bonds involve charged atoms (ions), while covalent bonds do not.

2. Covalent bonds share electrons, which causes them to bond more permanently. Ionic bonds are an attraction between opposite charges; ionic compounds dissociate in solution.

3. Metals generally have three or fewer electrons; therefore, they do not have enough to share, so they tend to donate their electrons.

4. If an atom gains electrons, it will become negative, if it loses electrons, it will become positive. The number of electrons gained or lost determines the charge of that ion.

5. No. Explanations may vary, but should be similar to the following: If there is only one hydrogen atom, it could not bond with three sulfur atoms because it only has one electron to share.

5. MAKING SOAP

Idea for class discussion: Ask two or three students to name their favorite soaps and explain why they prefer them. Discuss some of the different characteristics of soaps.

Note to the teacher: Soap molds can be made of milk or juice cartons. These do not need to be lined with wax paper since they are coated with wax.

Analysis

1. Answers may vary. Indications that a chemical reaction occurred may include color change, texture change, or change in pH.

2. The lye solution is generally clear, but may be slightly cloudy. The oils are generally transparent and yellowish (but may vary depending on the oils used). After mixing, the soap is opaque and usually a white, cream, or yellow color before any coloring is added.

3. The phenolphthalein should turn bright pink in the lye solution and either remain clear or turn pale pink in the soap solution. If this is not the case, too much lye was used and the soap will not be safe to use on the skin.

4. Answers may vary. The pH was lowered when the lye reacted with the oil. This is because it was a neutralization reaction and the solution turns from very basic to only slightly basic.

5. If too much lye is used, the pH of the soap will be too high and the soap will not be safe. If not enough lye is used, saponification may not occur and the mixture may not solidify.

6. OZONE DEPLETION

Idea for class discussion: Help students understand that ozone can be found in two general regions, the upper atmosphere where it plays a protective role and at ground level where it is a component of air pollution.

Analysis

1. See Figure 1 for O_2, and Figure 2 for O_3 (resonance structure).

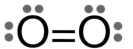

Figure 1

Structural formula for O$_2$

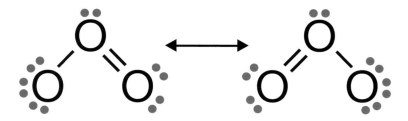

Figure 2

Structural formula for O$_3$

2. Oxygen is unstable as a single atom because it only has six electrons in its valence shell. Oxygen needs eight electrons in its outermost shell to be stable. With eight electrons it will bond easily so that it can attain that stability.

3. Oxygen is most stable as O$_2$; therefore, it will not react easily with other atoms, such as chlorine. However, O$_3$ is less stable because of its resonating electrons and it will react with chlorine.

4. Oxygen atoms are extremely reactive as single atoms. They are so reactive that they will "steal" the oxygen that is bonded with the chlorine.

5. There are three types of ultraviolet radiation: UVA, UVB, and UVC. UVC radiation is known as short wave radiation. It has a wavelength of 280–100 nanometers (nm) and diffuses easily when it hits most any gases within the atmosphere, so it rarely hits the Earth's surface.

   UVB radiation has medium wavelengths, being 315–280 nm. UVB radiation can cause sunburn, skin cancer, and eye damage, and it can destroy living tissue and DNA.

   UVA radiation has a longer wavelength of 400–315 nm. It penetrates deeper than UVB radiation does, but generally does not cause sunburn. It can, however, cause damage to DNA and deeper tissues within the skin and cause premature aging.

6. Answers will vary, but may include sunburn, skin cancer, damage to eyes, premature aging, health problems, damage to crops, and destruction of microorganisms.

7. Answers will vary based on student models.

8. Answers will vary.

7. CATALYSIS OF HYDROGEN PEROXIDE

Idea for class discussion: In small groups, have students discuss some of the evidences that a chemical reaction is taking place. Ask one or two groups to share their ideas. (Evidences of chemical reactions include fizzing or bubbling, production of heat or light, formation of a solid, disappearance of a solid, and change in color.)

Note to the teacher: If a burette, burette clamp, ring stand, and funnel are not available, you can substitute a 10–milliliter (ml) syringe.

Analysis

1. $2 H_2O_{2\,(aq)} \rightarrow 2 H_2O_{(l)} + O_{2\,(g)}$

2. Heterogeneous; it is a solid, while the reaction occurring is aqueous.

3. Answers will vary based on student observations, but will likely include descriptions of the bubbling that occurred in the reaction that contained the catalyst.

4. Potassium permanganate indicates the amount of hydrogen peroxide remaining in the solution. Without hydrogen peroxide, the potassium permanganate turns the solution from brown to deep purple.

5. Average values will vary based on student results.

6. Answers may vary, but generally more potassium permanganate is used in the uncatalyzed reaction, while a smaller volume is used to titrate the catalyzed solution.

7. The amount of potassium permanganate decreases as the reaction proceeds because the amount of hydrogen peroxide decreases.

8. WOOD ALCOHOL

Idea for class discussion: Most students are familiar with ethanol, the type of alcohol sold in stores. Point out that methanol is added to the product as a denaturant, rendering the alcohol unfit to drink.

Analysis

1. Answers will vary, but students should describe the appearance of wood before it was burned—tan color, hard, distinct pieces, etc.—and after it was burned—black, porous, crumbles easily, etc.

2. Answers may vary. The glassware generally turns yellow to brown because of the tar, or creosote, formed from the burning of wood.

3. When a match is placed in the mouth of the tubing, the gases escaping should ignite. This is because of the hydrogen gas and methanol vapor that are being produced.

4. No, methanol was not the only substance formed. Thick, dark–colored liquid tar forms at the bottom of the test tube. A mixture of acetic acid and methanol form a syruplike mixture in the tube, and pure methanol generally exists at the top of the test tube.

5. Answers will vary. See Figure 3 for an example. Tar is found at the bottom of the tube since it is the most dense. The methanol/acetic acid mixture (pyroligneous acid) forms above the tar, and any pure methanol will be found in the top layer of liquid.

6. Answers will vary based on student observations. The flame burns quickly and is a very pale color, which is almost invisible in the sunlight.

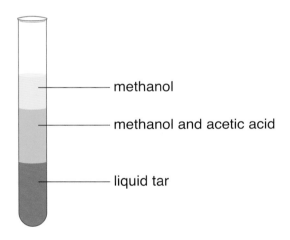

methanol

methanol and acetic acid

liquid tar

Figure 3

9. SOLUTES AFFECT THE BOILING POINT OF WATER

Idea for class discussion: As a demonstration before the experiment, heat a large beaker of water to almost boiling. Add salt and let students observe the results. Have them offer some explanations for what happened. Review their explanations after the experiment.

Analysis

1. Answers will vary based on student procedures. Students should state which solutes they chose to test in this experiment and explain why they chose those additives.

2. Answers will vary. Control factors could include using deionized water with no solute, using the same amount of water for each trial, and using the same amount of solute for each trial. It is important to maintain control variables in a scientific experiment to be sure that the results are due to the experimental variable only and not any other factors.

3. Answers will vary, but the temperatures for solutions with solutes should be higher than pure water. Substances that dissociated into a large number of particles raise the boiling point more than those that yield only a few particles.

4. Answers will vary based on student opinion. Students should describe why they feel that they got the results that they did in this experiment.

5. Sodium chloride (NaCl), two particles; sugar ($C_{12}H_{22}O_{11}$), one particle; calcium chloride ($CaCl_2$), three particles; potassium chloride (KCl), two particles; magnesium chloride ($MgCl_2$), three particles.

6. Graphs will vary, but all should show a trend of the temperature increasing as the number of particles increases, such as in Figure 4.

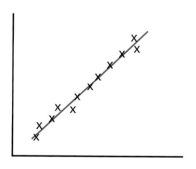

Figure 4

7. The boiling point increases as the number of particles increases.

10. POTABLE WATER

Idea for class discussion: Ask students what they would do for water if they were lost in the wilderness for several days. Discuss the problems they might experience from drinking water that is not purified.

Notes to the teacher: The First Alert™ test kit is recommended. In this kit, the tests are combined into four packets: bacteria, lead/pesticide, nitrate/nitrite, and pH/hardness/chlorine.

Analysis

1. Answers will vary based on the water sample used. Students should list all of the contaminants detected by the water test.

2. Answers will vary based on student opinion. Students should describe which method they think will be the most effective and include justification for their answer.

3. Answers will vary based on student results and the water sample used. Students should describe any visible changes in purity after the treatments.

4. Answers will vary based on student results and the water sample used.

5. Answers may vary. Boiling and chemical treatment are generally the most effective at removing microorganisms.

6. Answers may vary. Carbon filtration and chemical treatment are generally the most effective at removing chemical substances.

7. Answers will vary based on student opinion. Students should describe the process or combination of processes that would provide the safest and best–tasting water.

11. SOLUTIONS AND SPECTROPHOTOMETRY

Idea for class discussion: Prepare two different solutions of food coloring and water that are almost identical. Have students judge any differences in the colors of the solution. Point out that the human eye cannot assess color as accurately at a spectrophotometer.

Note to the teacher: Each group may be given a different unknown if desired, but the instructor should know the concentrations in order to check for accuracy.

Analysis

1. Answers will vary based on student observations; however, the solutions should range from clear to pale blue to deep blue as the concentration increases

2. Answers will vary based on student opinions. Students should predict which solution they think will have the highest absorbance and which will have the lowest and justify their answers.

3. The blank cuvette is used to calibrate the spectrophotometer and set a baseline, where pure water will absorb no light, so that when $CuSO_4$

is added, the readings will only reflect the absorbance due to adding the solute.

4. Graphs should have molarity on the X–axis and absorbance on the Y–axis. They should show a positive correlation between the two measurements similar to the one in Figure 5.

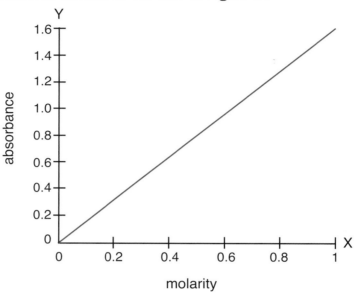

Figure 5

5. As the molarity increases, the absorbance of light increases as well.

6. Answers will vary based on student results and original hypothesis. Students should tell whether or not their predictions about the experiment results were accurate and explain why.

7. Answers will vary. Accuracy will be determined based on the molarity of the unknown solution prepared by the instructor.

8. Answers will vary. Results could be different from what was expected due to error in diluting solutions, impurities in the solutions, and smudges or fingerprints on the cuvette.

12. ENDOTHERMIC AND EXOTHERMIC REACTIONS

Idea for class discussion: Ask students to make a list of chemical reactions that produce heat and those that take up heat energy. Revisit the lists after the experiment.

Analysis

1. $Ba(OH)_2 + 2NH_4Cl \rightarrow 2NH_3 + BaCl_2 + 2H_2O$

2. Answers will vary, but most likely will include the evolution of ammonia gas (causing an odor), production of liquid substance from two powdered substances, and the change in temperature that occurs.

3. Graphs will vary but will most likely be similar to the one in Figure 6.

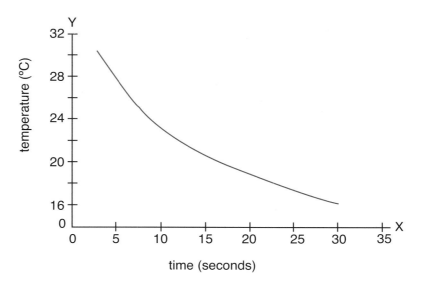

Figure 6

4. $Mg + 2HCl \rightarrow H_2 + MgCl_2$

5. Answers will vary, but will likely include the evolution of gas (bubbling), metal dissolving, and temperature change.

6. Graphs will vary but will most likely be similar to the one in Figure 7.

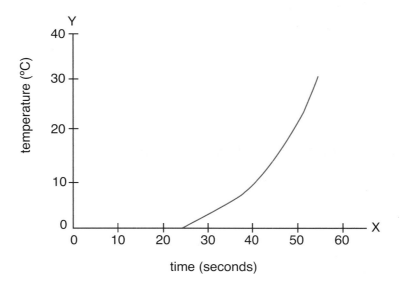

Figure 7

7. Answers will vary. Students should discuss the differences in graphs for the endothermic and exothermic reactions. The endothermic reaction should be a negative sloping line and the exothermic reaction will show a positive sloping line.

13. FINDING MOLAR MASS

Idea for class discussion: Review the concept of moles (mol). Ask students to explain what "1 mole" and "1 dozen" have in common.

Analysis

1. Answers will vary based on experimental data. Initial mass of lighter − final mass of lighter = mass of butane.

2. Answers will vary. The constant 0.0821 L*atm/mol*K will be used if the barometer measures in atmospheres, and 8.31 L*kPa/mol*K will be used if the barometer measures in kilopascals.

3. The partial pressure of water will vary based on the temperature. Use the data table on page 161 for water vapor pressure. The partial pressure of butane will be equal to the atmospheric pressure minus the vapor pressure of water.

4. Answers will vary based on experimental results *(ml/1,000 = L)*.

5. Answers will vary based on experimental results (°C + 273 = K).

6. Answers will vary based on experimental results (*n = PV/RT*).

7. Answers will vary based on experimental results (*M = m/n*).

8. The molar mass of butane is 58.12 g/mol.

9. Answers will vary based on experimental results. | experimental value − actual value | / actual value × 100 percent. (The absolute value of actual − experimental should be used to calculate the error, therefore the value will not be negative.)

10. Answers will vary. Some sources of error may include not drying the lighter completely before weighing it; releasing gas into the water container, not into the graduated cylinder; and inaccurate measurements of temperature, volume, or mass, etc.

14. CHEMICAL MOLES

Idea for class discussion: Review the concept of a chemical equation. Ask students to explain why an equation must be balanced.

Analysis

1. $NaHCO_3 + HCl \rightarrow NaCl + H_2O + CO_2$.

2. 1:1

3. Molar (M) mass of baking soda = 84.01 g/mol; M mass of sodium chloride = 58.44 g/mol

4. Answers will vary based on the exact amount of baking soda used. If exactly 2.00 grams (g) of baking soda are used, then 0.0238 mol of baking soda are used (2.00 *g* × 1 *mol*/84.01 *g*).

5. Answers will vary based on the exact amount used. However, since the mole ratio is 1:1, the number of moles of salt should be the same as the number of moles of baking soda (0.0238 mol, if exactly 2.00 g are used).

6. Answers will vary based on the amount used. If exactly 2.00 g of baking soda (0.0238 mol) were used, then 1.39 g of sodium chloride should be produced (0.0238 *mol* × 58.44 *g*/1 *mol*).

7. Answers will vary based on experimental results % yield = actual yield/theoretical yield × 100%

8. Answers will vary but may include the following: not driving off all of the liquid before finding the mass, losing solid product during heating, product lost during the initial bubbling reaction, and inaccurate measurements of mass before or after heating.

15. HEAT ENERGY

Idea for class discussion: Ask students to list some common fuels (for homes, cars, or appliances). Tell students that not all fuels are capable of releasing the same amount of energy. Ask them to explain why.

Analysis

1. Answers will vary depending on the fuels selected; methanol = 32.04 g/mol; ethanol = 46.07 g/mol; propanol = 60.10 g/mol; isopropanol = 60.10 g/mol; butanol = 74.12.

2. Masses will vary due to experimental conditions.

3. Moles of fuel used will vary based on the mass used (mol = mass/M mass).

4. Temperature change will vary based on experimental conditions; final temperature − initial temperature.

5. Values for *q* will vary based on experimental results. Students will use the equation $q = m \, C \, \Delta T$.

6. Answers will vary based on calculated heat value. All measurements in joules (J) will be divided by 1,000 to determine the kilojoules (kJ).

7. The calculated heat of combustion will vary based on experimental data. Students should use the equation: heat of reaction/moles of fuel. The units will be in kJ/mol.

8. Answers will vary based on experiment results. The compound with the largest M mass and more atoms will most likely have the highest heat of combustion because of the energy stored in bonds.

9. Actual values: methanol, 726 kJ/mol; ethanol, 1,368 kJ/mol; propanol, 2,021 kJ/mol; isopropanol, 2,021 kJ/mol; butanol, 2,671 kJ/mol; percent error = (actual value − experimental value/actual value) × 100 %.

10. Answers may vary. Possible answers may include the following: heat was lost to the environment, insulation was not sufficient, the water could have been heated unevenly, measurements were not taken carefully, etc.

16. CHLORIDE LEVELS

Idea for class discussion: Discuss the uses of chlorine bleach as a cleaner. Ask students how waste water high in chlorine bleach might be problematic.

Notes to the teacher: If the amount of silver nitrate in the burette is low at any point in the experiment, refill it and simply record the initial volume again.

Analysis

1. Answers will vary based on student speculations. Students should include an explanation for why they think the sample they choose will have the highest concentration of chloride ions.

2. Answers wll vary. Average volumes will vary based on experimental results.

3. Number of moles will vary based on experimental results. M = mol/ volume (liters [L]). Therefore, the number of moles will be equal to the M of silver nitrate (0.1 M) × the volume used in L.

4. $Ag^+ + Cl^- \rightarrow AgCl$. Mole ratio: 1 mole of Ag for every 1 mole of Cl.

5. Answers will vary, but should be the same as the moles of silver nitrate found in question 3.

6. Answers will vary based on experimental results. Students should include their opinion as to why they think that sample had the most chloride ions.

7. Answers will vary. Students should state whether or not their original hypothesis was accurate and give reasons why their original hypothesis could have been inaccurate.

17. THE RATE OF RUSTING

Idea for class discussion: Have students define rust in their own words and explain the causes of rusting.

Note to the teacher: Use iron wool, not steel wool, which resists rust. Make a 15 percent salt (NaCl) solution by stirring 15 g salt in 100 ml of distilled water; a 15 percent baking soda solution by stirring 15 g baking soda in 100 ml of distilled water; and a 50 percent vinegar solution by mixing equal part vinegar and distilled water.

Analysis

1. $2Fe + O_2 \rightarrow 2FeO$

2. Answers will vary based on solutions chosen. Students should explain the reasoning behind choosing the solutions that they did.

3. Answers will vary based on student procedures. Answers may include finding the change in mass due to corrosion, visual quantification of rust present, etc.

4. Answers will vary based on student results. Students should rank their solutions from lowest amount of rust to highest.

5. Answers will vary based on student results. Most likely, the strong acids/bases will cause the most corrosion and the distilled water will cause the least.

6. Answers will vary. Electrolyte solutions (those with dissolved ions) produce the highest rusting rates.

18. THIN LAYER CHROMATOGRAPHY

Idea for class discussion: Have students name some mixtures and some solutions, then ask them how they would separate the components of either. Explain that thin layer chromatography is a way to separate the components of a solution.

Analysis

1. The distance between the origin and solvent front will vary based on the length of the plates used and the distance the solvent traveled.

2. Answers will vary based on the solution used. Measurements should be made from the baseline to the center of each spot.

3. Answers will vary based on the solution used.

4. R_f values will vary based on the solution used, the solvent, and the laboratory conditions. Calculations should be made using the equation, R_f = distance solution traveled/distance solvent traveled.

5. Answers will vary depending on analgesics used. Typically, analgesics such as Excedrin™ contain acetaminophen, aspirin, and caffeine, Midol™ contains aspirin and caffeine, Tylenol™ contains predominantly acetaminophen, Advil™ is mostly ibuprofen, and Anacin™ is aspirin and caffeine.

6. Answers will vary. Some analgesics such as Aleve™ contain naproxen sodium, which was not in one of the standard solutions. Others may contain binding agents, flavorings, and coloring compounds.

7. Pen lines are made of ink, which is soluble in most nonpolar solvents. It will separate out during chromatography and interfere with the results of the experiment.

8. If too much solution is used, the dots on the plate will be smeared because there is too much of each component to make a spot. If not enough is used, the components may not be picked up in the solvent and separated.

19. LEVELS OF SUGAR

Idea for class discussion: Have each student write down the name of two beverages that they consider to be healthy choices. After the experiment, see if students want to change their choices. You might encourage students to consider that juices contain other nutrients (such as vitamin C) when deciding.

Note to the teacher: Be sure that the orange juice is the type that does not contain pulp. Prepare standard solutions before class. Each group will need 10 ml of each solution. A 5 percent solution is made of 5 g of sugar in 100 ml of distilled water, a 10 percent solution of 10 g of sugar in 100 ml of distilled water, and so on.

Analysis

1. Answers will vary based on student measurements. Density should be determined using the formula: density = mass/volume.

2. Graphs will vary based on density measurements, but the graphs should have a positive slope similar to the graph in the experiment (Figure 2 on page 135). All axes should be labeled and have an even scale, and the plots should be connected to create a curve.

3. Answers will vary based on student measurements. Density should be determined using the formula: density = mass/volume.

4. Answers will vary. The concentration values will vary based on the fruit juices used and their correlation with the calibration curve.

5. Answers will vary based on the juices chosen. Typically, apple, pear, and berry juices have the lower sugar concentrations while orange and grape juices have the higher sugar concentrations.

6. Answers will vary based on students' original predictions and the results of their experiments. Students should assess whether their predictions were accurate and tell why they were or were not accurate.

7. Answers will vary, but typically the amount of sugar on the label of juices is positively correlated to its sugar concentration.

20. MICROSCALE PERCENT COMPOSITION

Idea for class discussion: Explain to students some of the advantages of microscale procedures in the chemistry lab.

Note to the teacher: Sugar–free drinks work best for the percent composition calculations, because sugar is very heavy. If the drink is sugar–free, we will be able to assume that the mass of the solution is composed of only water and carbon dioxide.

Analysis

1. Answers will vary based on experiment data. Students should subtract the mass of the syringe from the mass of the syringe filled with the drink.

2. Answers will vary based on experiment data. Students should subtract the mass of the syringe from the mass of the syringe with the drink after the CO_2 was removed.

3. Answers will vary based on experiment data. Students should subtract the mass of the drink with CO_2 removed from the syringe with carbonated drink in it.

4. Answers will vary based on experiment data. Students should divide the mass of the water (the drink without CO_2) by the M mass of H_2O: mass of the water (g) / 18.02 g/mol.

5. Answers will vary based on experiment data. Students should divide the mass of the CO_2 by its M mass: mass of the CO_2 (g) / 44.01 g/mol.

6. Answers will vary based on experiment data. The ratio formula is: mol H_2O/mol CO_2.

7. Answers will vary based on experiment data. Students should multiply the ratio of water to carbon dioxide (from question 6) by 18.02 g/mol. The product should be added to 44.01 g/mol in order to obtain the M mass of the carbonated drink.

8. Answers will vary based on experiment data. Students should divide the mass of the carbon dioxide by the mass of the entire compound to obtain the percent composition: % composition = 44.01 g/mol/ molar mass of carbonated drink (from question 7) × 100 %

9. The gas was placed under a great deal of pressure to force it to dissolve into the liquid. Negative pressure causes gas to come out of solution because it creates open space for the gas to fill, drawing it out of the solution.

10. Gases stay dissolved in solution much more easily in lower temperatures, and they separate from the liquid more easily when it is warmed because molecules speed up when they are heated and are less likely to stay in a condensed liquid solution.

Glossary

activated complex in a chemical reaction, an intermediate product formed when reactants come in contact

activation energy minimum amount of energy required to initiate a chemical reaction

active site region on the enzyme where substrate(s) bond to the enzyme and a chemical reaction takes place

aeration process of mixing air with water that increases levels of oxygen in the water

alcohol group of organic chemicals that contains a hydroxyl (–OH) functional group

alkali metal one of the reactive metallic elements in group 1 of the periodic table

analgesic medication that relieves pain

anode positively charged electrode or region in a chemical reaction

benzene colorless, flammable, toxic organic compound obtained from crude oil found in many products, including glue and paint

biphenyl an aromatic organic compound that is a starting material in the product of polychlorinated biphenyls (PCBs)

bomb calorimeter sealed chamber for measuring the heat produced during chemical reactions

Boyle's law principle that when the temperature is constant, the pressure of an ideal gas varies inversely with its volume

buoyancy upward force that holds up a floating object

butane hydrocarbon (C_4H_{10}) found in natural gas

calorie unit of measurement used to represent the amount of energy in food

carboxylic acid an organic acid that contains at least one carboxyl (–COOH) functional group

carotenoids group of red, yellow, and orange pigments that are found in plants

catalyst chemical that speeds up the rate of a chemical reaction without being changed by the reaction

catalyze change the rate of a chemical reaction by use of a catalyst

cathode negatively charged electrode or region in a chemical reaction

cellular respiration aerobic process that occurs in cells' mitochondria in which glucose is changed to adenosine triphosphate (ATP)

chlorofluorocarbon organic molecule that contains carbon, fluorine, and chlorine, which was once used in aerosol cans and refrigerants

coefficient the number in front of a chemical formula in a chemical equation

colligative property property that depends on the number of particles in a solution rather than the chemical nature of the particles

combustion energy energy released during a combustion reaction

combustion reaction exothermic chemical reaction between a fuel and an oxidant

covalent bond chemical bond formed between two atoms by sharing electrons

creosote oily, flammable residue produced by distillation of wood tar

Dalton's law principle that the pressure exerted by a mixture of gases equals the sum of the pressures of the individual gases in the mixture

dehydration synthesis chemical reaction in which a water molecule is removed to build a compound

denature to change the chemical structure of a protein by heat, acid, or other agents

destructive distillation the heating of a solid such as wood in a closed container until it breaks down into its components

detergent synthetic cleaning agent that is not a soap but that acts as a surfactant to remove dirt and oil

disaccharide any carbohydrate made of two simple sugar molecules

distillation method of separating liquids by their different boiling points

electrolyte solution that contains free ions and conducts electricity

emulsifier substance that helps form an emulsion, a mixture of two or more substances that ordinarily do not mix

endothermic reaction chemical reaction in which heat is absorbed

enzyme protein that catalyzes chemical reactions in living things

equivalence point in titration, the point at which the moles of acid equal the moles of base in a solution

ester fruity smelling compound formed by the reaction of an alcohol and an acid

esterification chemical reaction between an alcohol and an acid that produces an ester

eutrophication process of increasing levels of nutrients in waterways, which results in increased growth of algae

exothermic reaction chemical reaction in which heat is released

fatty acid long chain of carbon atoms that makes up part of a triglyceride

fluoride ion of fluorine, an element in group 17 of the periodic table, which is added to drinking water in small quantities to prevent tooth decay

free radical a highly reactive atom (such as oxygen) or group of atoms with at least one unpaired electrons

freezing point temperature at which a liquid changes phases and becomes a solid

fructose a simple six–carbon sugar found in honey and fruit

glucose six carbon sugar found in cells where it serves as a source of energy for cellular respiration

glycerol colorless, odorless, syrupy liquid that serves as the backbone of a triglyceride

greenhouse effect process by which gases in the lower atmosphere trap heat before it can be radiated into space

groundwater water that collects beneath the Earth's surface

hard water water that contains a high concentration of mineral ions, especially calcium

heat energy of a substance associated with the motion of its molecules

heterogeneous made up of materials that are diverse

high blood pressure disorder in which the blood circulates through the arteries with too much force, damaging the arteries and increasing the risk of heart disease

homogeneous made up of materials that are the same

hydrogen bond force of attraction between oppositely charged regions of molecules

hydrometer instrument used to determine the specific gravity of a liquid

hydrophilic tending to interact with, or be attracted to, water

hydrophobic tending to repel, or not interact, with water

ideal gas hypothetical gas that obeys the gas laws of temperature and pressure

ion element or molecule that has an electrical charge because it has lost or gained electrons

ion exchange resin small, insoluble beads that attract hard water ions, such as calcium and release sodium ions

ionic bond chemical bond formed between two atoms when one atom loses electrons, becoming positively charged, and the other gains electrons, becoming negatively charged

kinetic energy energy of an object due to its motion

lactase enzyme that catalyzes the breakdown of lactose into its components

lime calcium hydroxide, a caustic material produced by heating limestone

lye caustic material, either sodium or potassium hydroxide, made by leaching wood ashes, which is used in making soap

metal any of several chemical elements that are shiny solids capable of conducting heat or electricity; an element that tends to lose electrons in a chemical reaction

micelle circular structure of lipid molecules in which the nonpolar parts are on the inside and the polar parts on the outside

molarity measure of the concentration of a solute in a solvent

mole the amount of a substance containing 6.023×10^{23} particles, the same number of units as there are atoms in 12 grams of carbon-12

nanometer unit of length equal to one–billionth of a meter

neutralization reaction reaction between a strong acid and a strong base that produces water and a salt

nonmetal any of several chemical elements that are poor conducters of heat and electricity and are brittle, waxy, or gaseous; an element that tends to gain electrons in a chemical reaction

octane a flammable hydrocarbon, $CH_3(CH_2)6CH_3$, found in many fuels

oleochemical chemicals that are derived from plants or animals

orbital region of space around a nucleus in which there is a high probability of find electrons

oxidation the combination of oxygen with a substance

oxidation reduction reaction (redox) chemical reaction in which one reacting substance loses electrons and is oxidized and another reacting substance gains electrons and is reduced

oxidize to combine with oxygen and form an oxide

ozone form of oxygen made of three oxygen atoms that is found in the stratosphere, where it filters out ultraviolet radiation

petrochemical chemical that is derived from oil or natural gas

pheromone chemical secreted by some animals that affects the behavior or body chemistry of other animals of the same species

photosynthesis biochemical process in chlorophyll–containing organisms in which light energy is converted to chemical energy of glucose

pigment   substance that produces a characteristic color

polar   having equal and opposite charges

polychlorinated biphenyls   group of toxic chemicals that were once used in the manufacture of electrical transformers

potable   safe for drinking

precipitate   separate by a chemical reaction that forms a solid in a liquid solution

product   the chemicals that are made during a chemical reaction

protozoan   mobile, single–cell eukaryotic organism that gets its food by ingestion

pyroligneous acid   liquid formed by the destructive distillation of wood that contains acetic acid, methanol, acetone, oil, and tar

reactants   substances that react with each other in a chemical reaction

reagent   substance or material used in a chemical reaction

refraction   the bending of light waves as they travel from one medium to another

refractometer   instrument used to measure the refraction of light in a liquid

reverse osmosis   process of filtration in which a watery solution or mixture is forced through a semipermeable membrane to remove impurities

saccharometer   type of hydrometer used to measure the concentration of sugar in liquids

saponification   process in which an ester is heated with a base to make soap

semipermeable membrane   membrane that allows the passage of some materials while preventing the passage of others

soda ash   common name of sodium carbonate, a base

soft water   water that contains few calcium or magnesium ions

solute   substance that can be dissolved by another substance

solvent   substance that can dissolve other substances

specific gravity   density of a substance compared to the density of water

specific heat   amount of heat required to raise the temperature of 1 gram of a substance 1 degree Celcius

spectrophotometer   instrument that measures the electromagnetic radiation of a substance

stratosphere   upper layer of the atmosphere between the mesosphere and the trophosphere

substrate   the substance on which an enzyme or catalyst reacts

sucrose   a 12–carbon sugar made from glucose and fructose that is produced by many plants and refined as table sugar

surfactant   substance that reduces the surface tension of a liquid

temperature   measure of how hot or cold a substance is

thin layer chromatography   method of separating mixtures using an inert substance, such as silica gel, as the solid phase and a solvent as the liquid phase

titration   method of finding the concentration of a reactant

triglyceride   lipid made of glycerol and three fatty acids

ultraviolet radiation   invisible energy with wave lengths that are longer than visible light but shorter than X–rays and that can damage living tissue

valence electrons   electrons located in the outer shell of an atom that are involved in chemical reactions

vapor pressure   the pressure exerted by a vapor; the tendency of a vapor to evaporate

visible spectrum   part of the electromagnetic spectrum the produces visible light

volatile able to evaporate easily at normal temperatures

xanthophyll   yellow, carotenoid pigments found in some plant and animal tissues

Internet Resources

The World Wide Web is an invaluable source of information for students, teachers, and parents. The following list is intended to help you get started exploring educational sites that relate to the book. It is just a sample of the Web material that is available to you. All of these sites were accessible as of July 2010.

Educational Resources

American Chemical Society. Periodic Table of the Elements. Available online. URL: http://acswebcontent.acs.org/games/pt.html. Accessed July 17, 2010. This interactive Web page is devoted to the Periodic Table and offers up–to–date information on elements and electron configurations.

Aus–e–tute. "Soaps and Saponification." Available online. URL: http://www.ausetute. com.au/soaps.html. Accessed July 17, 2010. Aus–e–tute is an online resource provided by teachers that includes an interactive tutorial on the chemistry of soap.

Bishop, Mark. *An Introduction to Chemistry*, 2010, Chiral Publishing Company. Available online. URL: http://www.preparatorychemistry.com/Bishop_Home.htm. Accessed July 17, 2010. This online textbook provides PowerPoint presentations, tutorials, and animations for a variety of topics in chemistry.

Centers for Disease Control and Prevention. Available online. URL: http://www.cdc. gov/. Accessed July 17, 2010. The CDC Web site provides information on water quality, microorganisms, and other topics related to health.

Chau, Sean. "Chemistry Phenomenon—Striped Toothpaste," 2010. SimpleChemConcepts. Available online. URL: http://www.simplechemconcepts.com/chemistry–phenomenon–striped–toothpaste/. Accessed July 17, 2010. This Web site by Sean Chua, a master chemistry coach, explains stripes in toothpaste and discusses the role of magnesium hydroxide in dental cleaning products.

Chem 1 Virtual Chemistry Textbook. "Getting Started," June 23, 2007. Available online. URL: http://www.chem1.com/acad/webtext/pre/index.html. Accessed July 17, 2010. This Web page provides information on several topics of basic chemistry, including properties of matter, energy, and units of measurement.

"Chemical Compounds Library," 2010. How Stuff Works. Available online. URL: http://science.howstuffworks.com/chemical–compounds–channel.htm. Accessed July 17, 2010. This Web site provides information on dozens of chemical compounds including esters and alcohols.

Department of Biochemistry and Molecular Biophysics, University of Arizona, "Chemistry Tutorial," 2003. The Biology Project. Available online. URL: http://www.biology.arizona.edu/biochemistry/tutorials/chemistry/page3.html. Accessed July 17, 2010. This Web site discusses the chemistry of water and other topics in chemistry.

Environmental Protection Agency. Available online. URL: http://www.epa.gov/. Accessed July 17, 2010. The EPA Web site has links to all topics relating to the environment, including loss of ozone in the stratosphere.

Farabee, M. J. "Reactions and Enzymes," June 6, 2007. Available online. URL: http://www.emc.maricopa.edu/faculty/farabee/BIOBK/BioBookEnzym.html. Accessed July 17, 2010. This chapter of Farabee's *Online Biology Book* provides information on how enzymes speed up chemical reactions and other topics related to biochemistry.

Francis, Eden. Introductory Chemistry Course Home page. Available online. URL: http://dl.clackamas.edu/ch105–00/. Accessed July 17, 2010. Eden Francis, the instructor for introductory chemistry at Clackamas Community College, provides notes on colligative properties, freezing point depression, vapor pressure change, and other topics.

Grandinetti, Philip J. "General Chemistry Lecture Notes," 2010. Available online. URL: http://www.grandinetti.org/Teaching/Chem121/Lectures/index.html. Accessed July 17, 2010. Grandinetti discusses many introductory topics including bonding, ions, electronegativity, and oxidation states.

Krantz, David, and Brad Kifferstein. "Water Pollution and Society," Available online. URL: http://www.umich.edu/~gs265/society/waterpollution.htm. Accessed July 17, 2010. The authors describe the sources of water pollution and discuss some of the techniques used to purify water.

Lower, Stephen. "Hard Water and Water Softeners," 2009. Available online. URL: http://www.chem1.com/CQ/hardwater.html. Accessed July 17, 2010. Lower explains how "hardness" minerals get in water and reviews techniques for water softening.

My Chemistry Tutor. Available online. URL: http://www.mychemistrytutor.com/. Accessed July 17, 2010. Teachers, professors, and other science professionals provide tutorials on this Web site for chemistry students who need a little extra help.

NASA. "Ozone Hole Watch," March 14, 2010. Available online. URL: http://ozonewatch.gsfc.nasa.gov/. Accessed July 17, 2010. This Web page provides daily updates on the status of the ozone hole.

Ozone Hole. "Arctic, Antarctic: Poles Apart in Climate Response," May 2, 2008. Available online. URL: http://www.theozonehole.com/arcticresponse.htm. Accessed July 17, 2010. This article explains how the two poles are responding differently to global warming.

Rader's Chem4Kids.com. Andrew Rader Studios, 2007. Available online. URL: http://www.chem4kids.com/index.html. Accessed July 17, 2010. Chem4Kids explains several chemical principles using simple language and colorful figures.

ScienceDaily. Chemistry Articles, 2009. Available online. URL: http://www.sciencedaily.com/articles/matter_energy/chemistry/. Accessed July 17, 2010. This extensive Web site provides links to articles on Lewis structures and other topics in chemistry.

Senese, Fred. General Chemistry Online, 2010. Available online. URL: http://antoine.frostburg.edu/chem/senese/101/index.shtml. Accessed July 17, 2010. Senese's Web site is designed for the freshman college student, but contains useful information for high school students including interactive tutorials and simulations.

Sibert, Gwen. Advanced Chemical Topics, July 5, 2004. Available online. URL: http://www.files.chem.vt.edu/RVGS/ACT/ACT–home.html. Accessed July 17, 2010. This Web page provides links, including a link to notes on a variety of chemical topics.

Skool. Chemistry, 2005. Available online. URL: http://lgfl.skoool.co.uk/keystage3.aspx?id=64. Accessed July 17, 2010. This Web site provides interactive tutorials on several chemistry topics including acids, alkalis, and neutralization.

Periodic Table of Elements

Key:

atomic number → 1
symbol → H
atomic weight → 1.008

Numbers in parentheses are the atomic mass numbers of radioactive isotopes.

1	2	3	4	5	6	7	8	9	10	11	12	13	14	15	16	17	18
1 H 1.008																	2 He 4.003
3 Li 6.941	4 Be 9.012											5 B 10.81	6 C 12.01	7 N 14.01	8 O 16.00	9 F 19.00	10 Ne 20.18
11 Na 22.99	12 Mg 24.31											13 Al 26.98	14 Si 28.09	15 P 30.97	16 S 32.07	17 Cl 35.45	18 Ar 39.95
19 K 39.10	20 Ca 40.08	21 Sc 44.96	22 Ti 47.88	23 V 50.94	24 Cr 52.00	25 Mn 54.94	26 Fe 55.85	27 Co 58.93	28 Ni 58.69	29 Cu 63.55	30 Zn 65.39	31 Ga 69.72	32 Ge 72.59	33 As 74.92	34 Se 78.96	35 Br 79.90	36 Kr 83.80
37 Rb 85.47	38 Sr 87.62	39 Y 88.91	40 Zr 91.22	41 Nb 92.91	42 Mo 95.94	43 Tc (98)	44 Ru 101.1	45 Rh 102.9	46 Pd 106.4	47 Ag 107.9	48 Cd 112.4	49 In 114.8	50 Sn 118.7	51 Sb 121.8	52 Te 127.6	53 I 126.9	54 Xe 131.3
55 Cs 132.9	56 Ba 137.3	57-71*	72 Hf 178.5	73 Ta 180.9	74 W 183.9	75 Re 186.2	76 Os 190.2	77 Ir 192.2	78 Pt 195.1	79 Au 197.0	80 Hg 200.6	81 Tl 204.4	82 Pb 207.2	83 Bi 209.0	84 Po (210)	85 At (210)	86 Rn (222)
87 Fr (223)	88 Ra (226)	89-103‡	104 Rf (261)	105 Db (262)	106 Sg (263)	107 Bh (262)	108 Hs (265)	109 Mt (266)	110 Ds (271)	111 Rg (272)	112 Uub (285)	113 Uut (284)	114 Uuq (285)	115 Uup (288)	116 Uuh (292)		118 Uuo (294)

*lanthanide series

57 La 138.9	58 Ce 140.1	59 Pr 140.9	60 Nd 144.2	61 Pm (145)	62 Sm 150.4	63 Eu 152.0	64 Gd 157.3	65 Tb 158.9	66 Dy 162.5	67 Ho 164.9	68 Er 167.3	69 Tm 168.9	70 Yb 173.0	71 Lu 175.0

‡actinide series

89 Ac (227)	90 Th 232.0	91 Pa 231.0	92 U 238.0	93 Np (237)	94 Pu (244)	95 Am (243)	96 Cm (247)	97 Bk (247)	98 Cf (251)	99 Es (252)	100 Fm (257)	101 Md (258)	102 No (259)	103 Lr (260)

Index

A

activation energy 47, 85, 86
alcohol 1, 3–6, 54, 55, 104, 108
alkali metals 30
American Dental Association 9
analgesic 123–127, 129
anode 120
Antarctica 45, 46
Arctic 46
aspirin 79, 123, 124, 125, 126
Avogadro's law 93

B

bacteria 67, 70, 71, 110, 143
boiling point elevation 64–65,
bomb calorimeter 108, 109
Boyle's law 93
butane 88–93

C

calibration curve 132–135
calories 131, 136
cancer 11
carbonated drinks 139–142
carbonation 138
carboxylic acid 1, 6
catalyst 47–51
cathode 120
cellular respiration 143
Centers for Disease Control 14
charcoal 57, 68
Charles' law 93
chloride ions 86, 110, 114, 115
chlorofluorocarbons (CFCs) 41, 43, 44

colligative property 64, 65
combustion engine 87
combustion reaction 102
condensation point 94
covalent bond 25, 26, 29, 30, 108
creosote 54
Cryptosporidium 72

D

Dalton's law of partial pressure 91, 93, 94
decomposition reaction 51
dehydration synthesis 1, 7
density 132–136
destructive distillation 54, 58
detergents 37, 38
distillation 16–19, 21, 56, 72, 115

E

endothermic reaction 81, 82, 85
Entamoeba 72
Environmental Protection Agency 67
enzymes 22, 37, 51, 52
equivalence point 115
ester 1, 4–7
exothermic reaction 81, 82, 85, 86, 87

F

fatty acids 37, 38
Fischer esterification 1, 6
flocculator 68
fluoride 9–15
free radicals 43, 44
freezing point depression 65

fructose 131, 135
fruit juice 131–135
fuel 102, 104, 105, 106

G

Gay–Lussac's law 93
Giardia 72, 73
global warming 44, 45
glucose 131, 135, 143
glycerol 37, 38
greenhouse effect 45
groundwater 21, 68

H

hard water 16, 20–22
hydrogen bond 60, 61
hydrometer 136

I

ideal gas equation 88, 92, 93
ion exchange resin 16, 17, 20
ionic bond 25, 26, 29, 30, 110

K

kinetic energy 81, 86, 94

L

Lewis structures 24, 25, 29
lock and key 51
lye 32–35

M

micelles 36, 37
molar mass 88, 92, 93, 99, 100, 106
mole ratio 96, 98, 100

N

neutralization reaction 32, 100

noble gases 30

O

octane 87

oleochemicals 37

oxidation 117

oxidation reduction (redox) reaction 51

ozone 40–42, 44, 45

P

paper chromatography 129, 130

percent composition 138, 142

percent yield 96, 100

petrochemicals 37

pheromone 7

photosynthesis 143

photosynthetic pigments 120

polar 36, 37, 121, 129, 130

pollution 67, 143

polychlorinated biphenyls (PCBs) 67

Priestley, Joseph 138

pyroligneous acid 58

R

refractometer 137

reverse osmosis 21, 115

R–group 1

rust 117–121

S

saccharometer 136

saponification 32, 38

soap 32–38

soft water 16

specific gravity 136

specific heat 102, 106, 107

spectrophotometer 74, 75, 76, 77, 79

stratosphere 40, 41, 44

sucrose 131–135

surfactants 37

T

thin layer chromatography (TLC) 123, 125–129

titration 48, 112, 113, 115

toothpaste 9–14

triglycerides 37

U

ultraviolet (UV) radiation 40, 41, 44, 80

V

valence electrons 24–27, 29, 30

van der Waals gas equation 94

vapor point depression 64–65

visible spectrum 79

W

water purification plant 68, 69

work 102